Transportation in America

DATE DUE			
MAR 2 0 1989			
JUN 0 2 1989			

TRANSPORTATION IN AMERICA

edited by DONALD ALTSCHILLER

THE REFERENCE SHELF

Volume 54 Number 3

THE H. W. WILSON COMPANY

New York   1982

THE REFERENCE SHELF

The books in this series contain reprints of articles, excerpts from books, and addresses on current issues and social trends in the United States and other countries. There are six separately bound numbers in each volume, all of which are generally published in the same calendar year. One number is a collection of recent speeches; each of the others is devoted to a single subject and gives background information and discussion from various points of view, concluding with a comprehensive bibliography. Books in the series may be purchased individually or on subscription.

Library of Congress Cataloging in Publication Data

Main entry under title:

Transportation in America.

  (The Reference shelf; v. 54, no. 3)
  Bibliography: p.
  1. Transportation—United States—Addresses, essays, lectures.   I. Altschiller, Donald.   II. Series.
HE203.T75   1982   380.5′0973   82-11190
ISBN 0-8242-0667-3

International Standard Book Number 0-8242-06673
PRINTED IN THE UNITED STATES OF AMERICA

CONTENTS

PREFACE 7

I. PROBLEMS AND PROGNOSTICATIONS IN
   TRANSPORTATION

Editor's Introduction 9
Michael Doan. The Great American Transportation
   Mess .... U.S. News & World Report 10
The Ways of Getting There .... Nation's Business 20
A Transportation Agenda for the 80s ....
   .... Transportation USA. 23
John H. Jennrich. How America Will Move Its People
   and Products .... Nation's Business 32
Tom Downs and Neil Goldstein. Transportation: The
   Roads (and Buses and Trains) from Here .... Sierra 43
C. Kenneth Orski. Public Enterprise and Public Trans-
   portation ....USA Today 50

II. AN ENVIRONMENTAL SOLUTION—RAILROADS

Editor's Introduction 58
William H. Jones. RAILROADS: Their Impact on Busi-
   ness in the Coming Decade .... Dun's Review
   Less Bumpy Track Seen for the 80s 59
   Overview 65
   Energy and Deregulation 71
Graham Beene. Where Are You, Benito, Now That We
   Need You? .... Washington Monthly 73
Barbara Rudolph. Deregulation of the Railroads ......
   .... Forbes 87

3

J. H. Foegen. Railroads: Out of the Past and into the
    Future .... Futurist   89

III. THE MASS TRANSIT ALTERNATIVE

Editor's Introduction   98
James O. Wheeler. Long, Long Trail to Work ....
    .... Geographical Magazine   99
Daphne Christensen. Autos and Mass Transit ....
    .... Vital Speeches of the Day   105
How Cities Are Coaxing People Out of Their Cars
    .... U.S. News & World Report   118
William J. Ronan. No Free Ride for U.S. Mass Transit
    Manufacturers ....
    Journal of the Institute for Socioeconomic Studies 124
Ellie McGrath. Rumbling Toward Ruin .... Time   137
James Kelly. Sick and Inglorious Transit .... Time   145
Joe Brady. No-Fare Transit—A Valuable Experiment
    AFL-CIO American Federationist   148

IV. TAKING CARE OF THE HANDICAPPED

Editor's Introduction   160
Jeannye Thornton. Equal Access—It Seemed Like a
    Good Idea .... U.S. News & World Report   160
Harrison Donnelly. Equality for Handicapped: Can the
    Nation Afford It? ....
    .... Congressional Quarterly Report   163

V. NEW WAYS TO SIGHTSEE

Editor's Introduction   172
Trolleys, Buses & Ferries—Great Ways to See the
    Sights .... Changing Times   172

Dewey Chiesl. Bicycles for Transportation ....
.... Bicycling 176
Horace Sutton. 80s Traveler: His Life and Future
Times .... Saturday Review 180
Samuel F. O'Gorman. How Will You Get Around
in 1991? .... Senior Scholastic 192

BIBLIOGRAPHY 199

"I travel not to go anywhere, but to go. I travel for travel's sake. The great affair is to move."
—Robert Louis Stevenson (1879)

Had the renowned Scottish novelist been able to travel in this country a century later, he would have been dazzled—if for nothing else, at least by the statistics. America can boast of 3.87 million miles of roads, 563,000 bridges, 117 million automobiles, 5 million motorcycles, 2,200 commercial and 200,000 private airplanes. Railroads carry 20 million passengers to more than 500 places while 52,000 buses and 15,000 rail cars transport more than 6 billion urban riders and commuters a year.

Transportation in America is a big business. Some economists estimate that the industry presently constitutes about 20 percent of the Gross National Product, and they forecast that by the end of the century, it may even comprise a larger share. Yet the American transportation industry suffers from no shortage of problems or critics. John Burby, for example, a former assistant to the Secretary of Transportation, grimly described the system as an "indifferent, inefficient, dirty, smelly, expensive, noisy and often destructive and deadly beast of national burden that goes where the spirit of speculation moves it or where it is driven by vested interest."

The problems of and prospects for American transportation are the subject of this compilation. The first section presents an overview of the current situation and predicts future developments.

Since the transcontinental railroad was completed in the mid-19th century, railroads have served as a crucial link in the American transportation web. The second section surveys economic and legislative issues pertaining to the financially plagued passenger and freight railroads.

7

Americans' virtual dependence on the energy-inefficient and environment-polluting automobile may be diminishing as cities around the nation devise transportation alternatives to the car. This is the subject of the third section. The next section examines the effects of federal legislation that provides for transportation needs of disabled Americans. The last section in the book discusses leisure traveling and future modes of transportation.

The editor wishes to thank the authors and publishers who have generously granted permission to reprint the articles in this volume.

DONALD ALTSCHILLER

April 1982

PROBLEMS AND PROGNOSTICATIONS
IN TRANSPORTATION

EDITOR'S INTRODUCTION

No transportation news seems like good news. Air travel is expensive and airports are not easily accessible. Automobile travel is no longer cheap either, as gasoline prices and repairs have soared in recent years. Nor is the appeal of motor vehicle travel enhanced by deteriorating interstate highways, crumbling municipal roads, and obsolete bridges. Railroad travel appears to be no better, as the traveler is hard-pressed to find reliable schedules and good service, even on federally-funded Amtrak on the Northeast corridor. In addition, mass transit in major cities certainly suffers from a number of ills, which range from crime-ridden subways to broken buses, while the beleaguered rider is overcharged for frequently long waits.

It is the "Great American Transportation Mess." This aptly-titled first article by Michael Doan in this section, reprinted from *U.S. News & World Report,* surveys the generally chaotic situation in the airlines, on the highways, on the railroads, and in mass transit. While it may be a mess, America does have an impressive system of highways and waterways and the article that follows, excerpted from *Nation's Business,* provides some transportation statistics in support of this. Current problems are not necessarily insoluble, cautions the third article from *Transportation USA,* "A Transportation Agenda for the 80s," which suggests possible solutions. A proposal by the U.S. Department of Transportation, the report provides a variety of policy guidelines, ranging from increasing fuel conservation programs to encouraging alternative methods for urban travel.

Looking beyond the 1980s, the National Transportation Policy Commission foresees about $4 trillion being spent on transportation by the end of the century. The essay from *Na-*

tion's Business, "How America Will Move Its People and Products," by John Jennrich, provides an economic analysis of future needs in transportation. Whether these needs can be met by now shrinking government subsidies for transportation remains to be seen. Tom Downs and Neil Goldstein, writing in *Sierra,* feel that the reduced government funds that will be appropriated should be spent to rehabilitate and maintain existing systems (transit and highway), rather than to expand them or build new ones.

Finally, C. Kenneth Orski's article, reprinted from *USA Today,* suggests that a decentralized, deregulated transportation system with greater private-sector involvement may provide less costly and more efficient service in the future.

THE GREAT AMERICAN TRANSPORTATION MESS[1]

For a public addicted to travel, the disruptions created by the air-traffic controllers' strike vividly demonstrate the vulnerability of the fragile transportation system that holds this country together.

Snafus in air travel are only the latest in a series of developments making it harder to get from home to places of work, study or play.

Highways and urban streets are falling into disrepair, sometimes dangerously so. City buses—even the newest ones—break down with startling regularity. Older subways are crumbling, and new systems are so costly that governments don't want to spend the money any more.

Passenger-train routes are skeletal remnants of what existed only two decades ago, and airlines, with their anemic profits, are hard pressed to replace aging, fuel-hungry fleets with modern equipment.

"Chronic shortage of funds is frequently blamed, but the

[1] Reprint of article by Michael Doan, with the magazine's domestic bureaus. *U.S. News & World Report.* 91:18–21. Ag. 31, '81. Copyright 1981, U.S. News & World Report, Inc.

fact remains that we have too often naïvely expected the future to take care of itself," says a "Transport Tomorrow" study sponsored by the Chamber of Commerce of the U.S.

The future hasn't taken care of itself, though, and each day brings new cracks in the nation's travel network. Just how deep does the damage run and what must be done to patch things up? From experts comes the following picture of a transportation system that is still one of the best in the world but whose future is in serious jeopardy.

Airlines: Cloudy Skies

Even before the air controllers' strike, travelers were plagued by higher fares, reduced service and crowded airports. The cost of jet fuel—up 900 percent in the past decade—has devastated airline-price policies.

Despite all the hoopla over discounts and price wars among airlines, the average plane fare has risen 30 percent in the past year, according to the Airline Passengers Association. In most routes, discounts are overshadowed by the big jumps in regular fares. For example, despite a discount fare as low as $149 from New York to Los Angeles—$10 less than the best discount five years ago—regular fares have skyrocketed from $198 to $438 over the same period.

Deregulation of airlines, begun by the Carter administration, has brought both benefits and problems. It has created more competition in popular routes, and many transportation authorities argue it makes economic sense for major trunk airlines to shift out of smaller cities, leaving those markets to commuter carriers.

Says Transportation Secretary Drew Lewis: "There are enormous amounts of fuel conserved when commuter lines expand because these firms are less dependent on large planes." One commuter airline advertises that its 150-mile flights burn less fuel than a Boeing 727 uses to warm up on the runway.

Still, for many passengers flying to or from these smaller cities, deregulation has led to delays, poorer service and additional connecting flights. Says John D. Kramer, Illinois secretary of transportation: "The number of airline seats available to downstate communities such as Springfield, Peoria and Champaign has declined 20 percent." In California, United Airlines and others used to offer $28 service from Bakersfield to San Francisco. But when United dropped that route after deregulation, a commuter airline ran the same service for $48, using smaller planes with fewer amenities.

Commuter airlines have been hit particularly hard by the strike, with traffic down 25 to 30 percent—a drop that analysts trace to the public's confusion over flight schedules and fears of delays and other problems.

Although the strike has reduced some of the crush, customers report that air travel has become increasingly tiring. The wait for baggage is longer in many cities, and as big-city airports expand, so do the distances that passengers must trudge to baggage areas or to airline gates. In addition, the growing number of short-distance flights has led to crowding and traffic delays in the busier airports. Flights in and out of Atlanta's airport, for example, rose from 556,992 in 1978 to 612,552 in 1980. The curtailed flight schedules imposed because of the strike have reduced the crowds, but there still is talk of expansion at massive O'Hare Airport in Chicago and of new airports in such cities as Denver and Los Angeles.

Expansion could be stalled, however, because of lack of funds. The federal government wants to cut its subsidies and make airports take on more of the load of new construction. It also wants Congress to boost the tax on fuel used by general aviation despite protests from owners of the nation's 208,000 private aircraft.

For the airline industry, the strike follows months of troubles. Major carriers lost a record 225 million dollars in 1980 as travel fell 3 percent and 41 percent of the seats went unsold. Some airlines blame price wars caused by deregulation for the earnings slump. All have been affected by the slump in the economy, which reduced both business and vacation travel. "In addition, lots of airlines were caught with gas-guzzling planes and found there was a lag time in getting equipment," remarks economist George E. Kroon of the First Interstate Bank of California.

The strike, though causing initial disruptions, could turn out to be a blessing for the airlines. It will be at least 21 months before enough new traffic controllers come on line to get air travel—now running at about 80 percent of pre-strike levels—back to normal. In the meantime, planes will carry fuller passenger loads, and airlines will drop unprofitable routes. Discount fares will be scarcer, too. Says one airline executive: "If people are banging on the doors to get tickets, there's no reason to offer big discounts."

Still, profits aren't expected to rise fast enough to allow carriers to make much progress in replacing aging fleets with new models, such as the fuel-efficient Boeing 767 unveiled August 4 [1981].

The estimated cost of revamping the fleet over the next five years is at least 4 billion dollars annually. Warns George James of the Air Transport Association: "If there are no new planes, airlines will have to reduce the size of the system and cut back service."

Highways: Potholes Galore

People who travel by car—and that's most Americans—can expect soaring expenses and crumbling pavements for years to come. The American Automobile Association figures that it now costs 24.8 cents per mile to own and operate a medium-sized car. In future years, damage inflicted by deteriorating streets and highways could rival high gasoline prices as a cause of spiraling car-ownership costs.

Consider these signs of the times—

—Truckers on Interstate 70 from Ohio to southwest Pennsylvania complain that potholes are so big they ruin their tires.

—Officials in Yuma County, Ariz., ripped up 250 miles of pavement and replaced it with gravel roads because it was cheaper than filling the potholes.

—New York City's Brooklyn Bridge had to be closed to traffic briefly in June after a cable snapped and killed a pedestrian.

—An Interstate 95 bridge outside Washington, D.C., is worn through so badly that it is possible to see the Potomac River through some of the cracks.

—San Francisco will need 1,000 years to fix its aging streets at the rate that they are now being rebuilt.

—Mackinac County, Mich., officials have stopped repairing roads entirely and are saving sparse funds for cleaning up snow during the winter.

Similar examples can be found almost anywhere, because America has built more roads and bridges than it can afford to keep. Streets in the typical urban area are so rippled and potholed that they make the highways seem like satin sheets. Finding funds to battle this deterioration may be next to impossible.

"There's very sad evidence that we're not taking care of our roads as rapidly as they deteriorate," says Tom Larson, Pennsylvania's secretary of transportation. "Our road systems have a life of 20 to 30 years, and many now have to be rebuilt."

As matters stand, the situation can only get worse, because roads will get a bigger beating than ever. Despite rising fuel prices, the National Transportation Policy Commission predicts a 69 percent rise in auto travel and a 142 percent increase in truck travel by the year 2000.

For the federal government, the biggest worry is the interstate-highway system, the 40,253-mile network of highways that was begun in 1956 to permit long-distance travel without stoplights and intersections. Construction expenses have gone up so much that it will cost nearly as much to complete construction of the final 5 percent of the system as it did to build the first 95 percent—65 billion dollars.

Maintaining the interstate highways will cost many times more. The highways were designed to go only 20 years without repairs, and few expected the beating they would take from heavy traffic. The backlog of immediate repairs needed in the system grew from 2.3 billion dollars in 1976 to 6.1 billion in 1980.

To make the interstate-highway surfaces adequate again and to keep abreast of the wear and tear will cost 16.8 billion dollars in the next decade, says the Transportation Department. However, Washington's highway spending is skewed to building new roads, and state governments are not budgeting nearly enough money to meet maintenance needs. As a result, estimates are that 9 percent of the interstate system is in serious disrepair, versus only 4 percent in 1975.

States cannot be expected to handle all of the cost. Says Donald J. Marttila, supervising highway engineer of the Federal Highway Administration: "If you're a state official and you're suddenly faced with 90 miles of four-lane road to maintain, it's not likely you'll get an automatic increase in your budget to maintain it."

To pay for repairs, states count on the gasoline tax, but revenues are going down rather than up. Don Ivey of the Texas Transportation Institute explains why: "Gasoline taxes are at a given rate per gallon. The actual number of gallons sold in the past few years has been declining because individuals are curbing their driving and driving vehicles that get better mileage. Therefore, gasoline taxes have not risen proportionately to the number of vehicles."

To catch up, 40 states are trying to raise fuel taxes. In Ohio, officials hope to end a two-year freeze on construction of new roads by boosting the tax from 7 cents to 10.3 cents this year and to 12 cents by March, 1983.

Also haunting cities and states is the 41-billion-dollar price tag for fixing obsolete and deficient bridges. The government reports that 4 out of every 10 highway bridges are deficient—restricted to light vehicles, closed to traffic or needing immediate repair.

Officials note that bridges are closed before they are dangerous, but that step creates other problems. Because the Sewickley Bridge across the Ohio River in southwestern Pennsylvania has been closed, fire equipment has been unable to cross the bridge, and ambulances have had to make a 10-mile-detour. A bridge over the Mississippi River between Prairie du Chien, Wis., and Marquette, Iowa, reopened August 12 after being out of service for seven months. While the bridge was closed, residents had their choice of a 67-mile detour to the next bridge or ferry service for which waits often ran 2 hours.

Amtrak: Is It Here to Stay?

A decade after the government assumed responsibility for running passenger trains, the trains themselves are much improved. But Amtrak, as the National Railroad Passenger Corporation is known, is inundated by red ink.

This year Amtrak is costing the federal government 881 million dollars in subsidies—roughtly $44 for each of the 20 million people buying tickets. Since its beginning in 1971, Amtrak has spent nearly 7 billion of government money to stay afloat and to replace its run-down fleet of cars and locomotives. But the price of these subsidies has been to make the passenger train a political football for both its proponents and critics.

Time after time, Congress has vacillated. One year it will appropriate money to add new routes; the next it will take the money away. Its subsidy has made Amtrak the target of budget cutters in every administration since its creation. Twice before and again this year, Presidents sought vast reductions in Amtrak's 24,000-mile route structure. Each time they largely failed, partly because of opportune gasoline shortages and partly because the people who depend on passenger trains made their voices heard in Washington.

Attempts to cut Amtrak back to just a few high-density routes are certain to continue so long as the public corporation is so heavily dependent on government. "On some routes, the government would save money if it were to discontinue service and simply purchase air-coach-fare tickets for passengers," says the Chamber of Commerce's transport study.

Those wanting to slim down Amtrak say that intercity

buses are a good alternative, serving 15,000 communities instead of Amtrak's 500 and not depending upon Washington for direct operating subsidies. Ridership on intercity buses rose 4 percent last year, with many small charter lines reporting booming business. But further deregulation of buses, should it occur, could mean reduced service for smaller communities. "Greyhound and Trailways are posturing themselves to become mainline carriers and drop smaller, unprofitable lines," observes Pennsylvania transportation chief Larson.

Railroad advocates argue that buses and airlines are subsidized by the government, too, though indirectly. "We're the only country in the world that asks our passenger rail system to make a profit," says Barry Williams, assistant director of the National Association of Railroad Passengers, a rail-consumer group.

Even with its problems, Amtrak is better off today in several respects. Equipment is either new—built since 1975—or completely rebuilt. With new cars and new engines up front, Amtrak's on-time record regularly approaches 90 percent. Ridership is up, too. Since 1972, Amtrak's first full year, passenger-miles—one passenger carried 1 mile—have risen 50 percent. People are now being turned away.

That's what happened to thousands of would-be air travelers who phoned Amtrak for tickets after the air controllers walked out. Those who could get through to jammed reservation centers were told that most long-distance trains were booked solid, and had been for weeks and sometimes months. "Our problem isn't having enough passengers to fill the seats; it's having enough equipment to satisfy the demand," says Amtrak President Alan S. Boyd. "During peak periods, Amtrak could easily fill the seats of another 300 rail cars a day."

While others predict Amtrak's demise, Boyd contends that passenger trains are headed for a renaissance. "Air travel is becoming increasingly expensive and inconvenient," he says. "Smaller automobiles are uncomfortable for long trips, and gasoline will be more and more expensive."

Mass Transit: Money Squeeze

Traveling across town without a car is becoming harder than ever as transit fares keep climbing and buses and subways fall into disrepair.

In cities everywhere, cash-starved governments can't keep up with demands by travelers for frequent, well-routed service. This summer, fares in Atlanta, Baltimore, Orange County, Calif., Minneapolis, Oklahoma City and Phoenix rose from 50 to 60 cents. In Chicago, transit prices rose from 80 to 90 cents and in San Jose from 35 to 50 cents. Rush-hour fares in Denver soared from 50 to 70 cents.

Financing problems are reaching such proportions that systems in several cities are in danger of bankruptcy, and new projects are at a standstill.

The biggest casualty is the modern subway system, hailed only two decades ago as the answer to urban transportation problems. "I have a feeling that because of the cost of things, large, new subway systems in the next 20 years will become a thing of the past," predicts Transportation Secretary Lewis.

Huge cost overruns in the two biggest new systems have made planners in other cities leery. In Washington, D.C., what started as a 2.5-billion-dollar subway network is mushrooming into what may be an 8.3-billion project. The San Francisco-Oakland system ended up costing 1.7 billion, more than double the original estimate.

There also are nagging technical problems. The San Francisco system is described as "overautomated" by Brian Cudahy of the Urban Mass Transit Administration. When a subway breaks down at one station, it can stall other trains miles away. In that city and in Washington, the computerized farecard systems are causing trouble. Tourists and commuters are often baffled by a set of card-dispensing machines—which frequently malfunction—that they must go through to pay their fares.

What's more, the Reagan administration refuses to boost funds for transit systems from the 3.9-billion-dollar level that prevailed in the fiscal year ending September 30. Most of the money will go to bus and trolley systems and to subway projects already under way. Federal budget planners say they won't pay operating costs for any system.

Especially hard hit by the cutbacks are subway projects planned for Los Angeles and Houston, where populations are growing far more rapidly than their transit systems. Los Angeles-area officials counted on the federal government to pay 80 percent of the cost of an 18.6-mile rail line linking central Los Angeles with the San Fernando Valley, but now they are gloomy about the system's future. Clogged traffic on the region's freeways and streets makes rapid transit essential, says Los Angeles transit official Barry Engelberg. "Buses cannot take it any more," he says.

In Atlanta, 12 miles of a new subway are operating, but officials say it may take until 1990 to build two extensions because of the federal cutbacks.

Systems built years ago are having troubles as well. The Regional Transportation Authority in Chicago came close to bankruptcy at midsummer, but continues to limp along with stopgap funds. At one point in June, the entire subway and bus system nearly shut down for lack of funds.

In New York, fares have risen from 35 to 75 cents in the past six years, but costs are only part of the problem. The real reason subway ridership is declining is the deteriorating cars and tracks. The number of breakdowns rose from 43,683 in 1979 to 71,773 in 1980, according to the city's Permanent Citizens Advisory Committee. "The picture which emerges is one of a system in physical collapse," says committee chairman Michael Gerrard.

Bus systems in smaller cities also are having trouble making ends meet. Officials in Birmingham, Ala., closed the entire bus system for three months last winter when they could not get local, state or federal aid. In Memphis, $500,000 thought to be earmarked by the Legislature for mass transit is being spent by the city to repair streets, while bus service deteriorates.

Looking ahead, the administration is casting a more favorable eye on light-rail systems, or long-distance trolleys, such as the one that opened in July in San Diego. Dubbed the "Tijuana Trolley," the line runs along railroad right of way from San Diego to the Mexican border. The system cost 86 million dollars to build, funded entirely by the state gasoline tax and a local sales tax. At 5 million dollars a mile, it was far cheaper than the 34 million per mile spent in San Francisco or the 43 million in Washington.

More experts are looking at the bus as the most efficient form of mass transit, especially when used on special lanes to avoid tie-ups with auto traffic. Says Randall Pozdena of the Federal Reserve Bank of San Francisco: "Even if a special lane must be built to accommodate express buses, its cost would be far lower than rail transit." Among the cities experimenting with new bus routes is Pittsburgh, which opened a 4.5-mile separated busway in 1977 and will open another 6.8-mile route next year. Not only do commuters get to their destinations quicker, but the city saves money by carrying more people with fewer buses in a fraction of the time it took when the buses traveled on the same streets as cars.

Experts predict, however, that projects like the Pittsburgh busways will be tougher to fund, since an important financial partner—the federal government—will be stingier with its aid. As with an increasing number of essential services, the burden will fall on private companies, local authorities—and the general public—to find new ways to ease the nation's transit ills.

THE WAYS OF GETTING THERE[2]

Transportation in America is a jigsaw puzzle with a million pieces—and a billion-dollar price tag.

Last year, the transportation system made up about 20 percent of the gross national product, or more than $415 billion, and involved about 20 percent of the labor force, or about 20.5 million workers.

Today, the parts of the system look like this:

[2] From *Nation's Business.* 67:40. N. '79. Reprinted by permission from Nation's Business. Copyright 1979 by Nation's Business, Chamber of Commerce of the United States.

Highways and Motor Vehicles

There are 3.87 million miles of roads, 81 percent of which are paved. Of the total, which has increased only 20 percent in nearly 60 years, nearly 3.2 million miles are in rural areas and 683,000 are in urban.

The Interstate Highway System, a projected 42,500 miles, is 93 percent completed. However, the system was begun in 1956, and now more than half of what has been built needs to be upgraded.

The total road system includes more than 563,000 bridges, with most travel over the 248,000 bridges on the major federal-aid system roads. More than 105,000 bridges, including nearly 40,000 major system bridges, are structurally deficient or functionally obsolete. About 72 percent of all the bridges were built before 1935.

Vehicles traveling on these roads and bridges include more than 117 million automobiles, 31 million trucks, five million motorcycles and 500,000 buses. By 1980, says the National Transportation Policy Study Commission, 90 percent of the eligible population could be registered to drive.

Air

There are 11 domestic trunk air carriers and eight local service airlines. There are about 2,200 commercial aircraft, down in number from 1970 but significantly faster and bigger. There are also 199,000 private aircraft. In 1978, 280 million airline passengers traveled to 620 commercial points of service. Of the 14,574 airports in the nation, 428 have Federal Aviation Administration air traffic control towers. Domestic air freight serves 9,000 U.S. communities.

Pipelines

There are 440,000 miles of oil pipelines, 255,000 miles of gas pipelines, and 400 miles of coal slurry pipeline.

Water

Waterborne commerce travels in three basic types of vessels: Inland vessels, mainly tugs and barges drawing nine feet or less; Great Lakes ships with a maximum draft of 25½ feet; and oceangoing ships, which generally have a draft of 35 feet or more.

There are 25,543 miles of inland waterways, including 170 dams and 255 locks, carrying 4,400 towboats and tugs and 28,-700 barges. The Great Lakes fleet numbers 150 bulk carriers and nine tankers. There are about 575 oceangoing ships including 214 flag vessels in the U.S. domestic ocean fleet; their average age is 21 years, double the age of the average international trade vessel.

The United States has 2,401 marine terminals, although only 170 are considered major commercial ports, and 50 get 87 percent of all commerce.

Rail

Amtrak passenger service carries 20 million passengers a year over 24,000 miles of track to 532 locations, using 350 locomotives and 2,000 railcars. Freight, 673 billion ton-miles in 1975, was hauled over 200,000 miles of track, using 27,700 locomotives—200 electrics, 11 steam, the rest diesel—and 1.7 million railcars, including 354,000 for coal.

Urban Transit

The industry, which has declined significantly since just after World War II, now carries more than six billion passengers a year in 52,000 buses, 11,300 railcars, and 4,340 commuter railcars.

A TRANSPORTATION AGENDA FOR THE 80s[3]

During the decade of the 1980s, more than $2 trillion will be spent on transportation in the United States.

The federal government will spend about $235 billion, state and local governments around $350 billion and private industry the other $1.5 trillion.

"While federal expenditures will be a small part of overall investment for the transport system in this decade, they will be very important to the structure and development of that system," says [former] Secretary of Transportation Goldschmidt in the DOT report, *Transportation Agenda for the 1980s: Issues and Policy Directions.*

"The need to carefully select these investments in the transport network requires the attention of the nation. We can, working together, seize upon opportunities which have been made clear in the wake of major resource, economic, and population changes of the 1970s."

The report points out that we are at the end of an era of cheap and abundant resources and at the beginning of a decade in which petroleum and other natural resources will be increasingly scarce and costly. These changes will force us to revise many of our assumptions about transportation priorities, America's place in the world market, and government/industry relationships.

As it makes transportation decisions and investments for the decade ahead, the government should be guided by four time-tested principles:

—Increased productivity and hard work are the essential ingredients that must drive the transportation sector in the 1980s.

—Maintaining and rebuilding our physical and industrial plant will be the key to long-term growth and economic stability.

[3] Reprint of staff-written article. *Transportation USA.* 7:2–6. Fall '80. Reprinted by permission.

—The conservation and stewardship of our natural and manmade resources are fundamental.

—Teamwork and cooperation among diverse interests— citizen groups, government, labor, and private industry—can and must shape the whole of the nation's transportation system.

This report, says Goldschmidt, "presents a brief view of some—not all—of the broad issues that confront us. It does not specify solutions. Rather, it is the beginning of a continuing dialogue directed at developing solutions to the challenges of this decade."

Energy

THE PROBLEM

During the first five months of 1980, U.S. consumption of oil dropped by 9.7 percent and gasoline usage has declined to its lowest level since 1971. Despite this improvement, our oil import bill is still equivalent to sending $10.6 million abroad every hour.

This excessive dependence on foreign sources of oil threatens the nation's future. It leaves us vulnerable to foreign blackmail and supply interruptions; it creates a balance of payments problem that destabilizes the dollar; it threatens our economy, including the loss of jobs as industry struggles to adjust to increasing oil prices.

Unless we continue to take corrective measures in the transportation sector, U.S. dependence on foreign oil—already 42 percent—will grow through the decade, with the likelihood of severe shortages.

THE POLICY DIRECTION

To get us through the immediate transition from an energy-rich society to one of increased price and unpredictable supply, we must turn to the lowest-cost, most readily available solution we can find—conservation.

Since 90 percent of all vehicle miles traveled are by auto, conservation efforts in the 1980s must focus on the auto and personal transportation. We must continue our efforts to build smaller fuel-efficient automobiles.

Federal, state, and local transportation officials should continue efforts to conserve fuel, such as corporate vanpools, ridesharing, shared-ride taxi, and corporate-subsidized buses. Taken together, actions by private citizens to conserve transportation energy will be the single most effective solution to America's petroleum problem.

But conservation efforts alone will not solve our energy problems. We should press forward with the development of promising new technologies to cut back our dependence on foreign oil—production of fuels from alternative sources, the development of a variety of non-petroleum-powered vehicles, and development of reduced crude oil recovery techniques.

Productivity

THE PROBLEM

The United States and the world are in the midst of a tenacious inflationary crisis that threatens our economy. At the core of this problem are the exorbitant price increases in oil, reduced investment, and a serious decline in productivity.

The decline in productivity has been pronounced in transportation, where the average annual rate of productivity growth fell from 2.9 percent in the period between 1965 and 1973 to 0.9 percent during the 1973–1978 period.

THE POLICY DIRECTION

To combat inflation, waste, and inefficiency in the transportation sector, the federal government must develop long-range conservation and capital investment strategies aimed at protecting our massive investments in the nation's transportation system and making more effective use of it.

Specifically, we must:

—arrest the deterioration of the nation's system of highways and make highway investments that will increase productivity, particularly in the elimination of bottlenecks, provide more efficient connections to ports, and seek low-cost solutions to traffic demand

—make it easier, through the Motor Carrier Act of 1980, for trucking companies to enter the business, expand their services, and raise or lower freight rates, and also resolve the complex issues of uniform truck size and weight limits

—allow the railroads to compete with other modes without the imbalance created by indirect government subsidies, to generate and attract capital vitally needed to improve service and productivity, and to cease operations or abandon unprofitable lines

—establish fare policies for public transit that decrease government operating subsidies, and concentrate on the costs generated by low-density routes and service, giving serious consideration to alternatives to conventional bus transit in low-density areas

—resolve the issue of the levels of federal subsidies to be given to the barge industry and to its principal competitors, the railroads and the trucking industry, and the issue of future capacity levels for inland waterways.

World Trade

THE PROBLEM

We have entered a new era in which our economy is increasingly linked to the world economy; in which energy, critical natural resources, and capital have become scarce and increasingly expensive; in which other developed nations have become highly competitive in a wide range of industrial products, including those connected with transportation.

Our position in this emerging world is a precarious one. Not only are we importing far too much oil; we are exporting far too many jobs as we surrender more and more of our basic industrial economy and markets to foreign competition.

In the early 1950s, this country produced more than 75

percent of the world's autos—today, that is less than 30 percent; more than 75 percent of the world's tires—today, less than 30 percent; more than 50 percent of the world's steel—today, 20 percent; and 50 percent of the aluminum—today, 25 percent.

THE POLICY DIRECTION

Improving our nation's performance in world trade is the surest path to achieving the goals of stabilizing the dollar and increasing job opportunities for Americans.

The transportation sector will have a key role in accomplishing this goal. Government, industry, and labor should confront the challenge with a new set of goals. We should:

—seek to export a greater volume of finished products, coal, and agricultural commodities

—assure that we have a transportation system—barge, pipeline, truck, rail, and aviation—able to support the flow of commerce required by expanded exports

—strive to remove the waste and inefficiency in transportation that add unnecessary expense to export products, particularly agricultural

—promote American technological leadership in the world transport sector marketplace.

It is also true that worldwide economic stresses during the 1980s could produce wasteful trade wars and other international problems. To avoid this, the government, including the Department of Transportation, must give greater attention to international cooperative efforts.

Transportation Manufacturing Industries

THE PROBLEM

Our transportation industry in the 1980s will be increasingly challenged to compete for domestic and world markets by foreign concerns with fresh technology, ample capital, economies better conditioned to high energy costs, and products backed by government policies designed to capture foreign markets.

Our auto industry is ailing—one out of four auto workers is unemployed; many plants have closed their doors. To survive and assert world market leadership, American manufacturers will have to spend billions to retool between now and 1985.

U.S. aircraft manufacturers, while still supreme in the world, are being seriously challenged by foreign competitors with energy-efficient products. These manufacturers must also contend with the implications of a growing shortage of materials for aircraft construction, the existence of only two large aircraft forging companies, and the need for alternative fuels research.

A clear message about national demand for transit equipment and the assurance of a reliable, steady flow of orders is essential to help restore full production levels by transit manufacturers.

The policy direction

What is required is a retooling by transportation equipment manufacturers to produce highly fuel-efficient vehicles of a variety of types, including technologically innovative vehicles suitable for personal travel, ridesharing, paratransit, and public transit.

Federal transportation programs should be used to stimulate private investment in transport-related and transport-dependent industries. A decade-long transportation investment program should be developed that will assure a nationwide pattern of public and private sector investments.

Mobility

The overview

The 1980s will see an expanding population with more

working women, more households, more elderly, more immigrants. While more households will locate in the city, the greatest population growth will be in the suburbs, small communities, and low-density areas where there is a high dependency on automobile travel.

A principal issue of the 1980s will be how to maintain mobility for all segments of the population in the face of severely increasing transportation costs and uncertainty of fuel supplies. These factors require us to improve the flexibility of our transportation system and to offer greater choice and diversity in transportation services.

THE POLICY DIRECTION

A major challenge of the 1980s will be to use our automobiles in more efficient ways. We need to capture the enormous potential that exists for expanded ridesharing and vanpooling.

Transportation planning in the 1980s should encompass a variety of paratransit modes, improved walking and bicycling systems, various types of buses, modern rapid transit, regional rail systems, and light rail systems.

Highway planning and transit planning must be integrated and related to the state, regional, district, and neighborhood planning efforts now in place or emerging.

Special effort should be directed to tackling the problem of personal mobility in small communities and rural areas where there is near-universal dependence on the automobile.

In the 1980s, public policy should encourage a shift from the single-occupant auto to alternative forms of transportation in intercity travel. Major public policy questions center on the competitive relationship between rail, bus, and air carriers, and on the amount of public subsidy that should be provided to Amtrak. The role of the Department must be to ensure that federal funds will be invested in areas that will yield the highest transportation benefits for society.

Community Revitalization

Population migration

Major population shifts are creating new patterns of growing and declining communities that will have profound consequences for transportation policy.

The South and West will continue to absorb floods of people and capital. The problem here will be how to expand the system to accommodate new growth, how to serve the mobility needs of people in low-density areas where conventional public transit systems are less productive.

In the Northeast and Northcentral states, the problem will be how to restructure the system to deal with stagnation or decline—disinvestment, accelerated deterioration, replacement needs, and maintenance needs.

The policy direction

We must find ways to avoid consigning still-useful building, labor, and land to the dust heap while they are potentially productive; ways to cushion the blow for displaced workers and make finding a new job easier; ways to assist distressed Northern cities in providing transportation to a population less and less able to pay. We should reconsider the wisdom of apportionment formulas, based on population, for allocation of urban transportation funds.

In the 1980s, the challenge will be to use transportation to improve the quality of life.

Other Issues

Transportation safety

We must provide greater incentives for industry, the states, and the private sector to act on the overall national concern of safety. All regulations, existing and proposed, must be carefully examined to assure that we are issuing the most effective regulations and that their consequences are understood.

AIR QUALITY

Most major urban areas will be unable to meet national ambient air quality standards by 1982 and will probably seek an extension of the compliance deadline. While failure to meet these standards involves continuing public health problems of significant magnitude, the dates for achieving urban air quality goals in some areas may need to be deferred. However, the goals themselves need not, and should not, be changed for transportation reasons.

NOISE

Increasingly effective solutions to traffic and aviation noise problems will be needed. In aviation, the problem of the conflict between two federal goals—energy conservation and aviation noise reduction—will need to be resolved. Since there is little economic incentive for the airlines or other transportation entities to reduce noise, control can be assured only with government regulation.

Departmental Requirements

To deal effectively with the issues on the national agenda, the Department of Transportation must improve its own organizational effectiveness. We must approach the future with a well-defined set of goals and a clear understanding of where our policies are leading us.

In the coming months and years, the Department of Transportation must turn to the task of responding to these and other transport issues of national concern.

HOW AMERICA WILL MOVE ITS PEOPLE
AND PRODUCTS[4]

How will Americans get where they're going in the year 2000? The federal government has spent $5 million over two years to find out. The answer: Not much differently than they do today.

There will be some changes in the ways America moves its people and its products, but very little of the futuristic transportation found in science fiction novels will materialize. The nation will still run on wheels, wings, tracks, and water. The primary changes will be in fuels—more diesel and synthetic gasoline—and in transportation costs.

The government's report, prepared by the National Transportation Policy Study Commission, forecasts a capital investment of $4 trillion between now and 2000 to keep a growing America moving. Representative Bud Shuster (R.-Pa.), commission chairman, warns that the "world's best transportation system is in danger" because it may not be able to meet future needs.

"The present level of public and private investment will not preserve the existing system," he says. "The demand for transportation will grow dramatically, outdistancing the rate of population growth by nine times for freight and four times for passengers. Government over-regulation is inhibiting the return on investment necessary to attract capital for future growth."

Representative Shuster's pessimistic alarm is echoed by Peter G. Koltnow, chairman of the Transportation Research Board, an arm of the National Academy of Sciences. He thinks the nation's highway system is living on borrowed time.

"The gap between highway needs and expenditures will grow substantially by 2000 unless our national transportation

⁴ Article by John H. Jennrich, staff writer. *Nation's Business.* 67:35–40. N. '79. Reprinted by permission from Nation's Business. Copyright 1979 by Nation's Business, Chamber of Commerce of the United States.

priorities are changed," he says. "Federal, state, and local governments are all going to have to deal with deteriorating highways.

"The report of the National Transportation Policy Study Commission shows that if we want a better system or even the status quo in the years ahead, we are already behind schedule in preparing for it," adds Mr. Koltnow, who is also president of the Highway Users Federation. "Although the public has come to expect a good road system, the report clearly shows that we are in danger of losing it."

Optimistic About Impact

The commission's deputy executive director, John W. Fuller, is optimistic about the report's impact. He says it describes "moderate ways to make incremental changes." One or more congressional bills will result from the report, he predicts. Even with the big aggregate numbers, the cost of transportation as a percentage of family and national budgets is expected to decline.

But, Dr. Fuller adds, even if all the changes sought by Representative Shuster and the other commissioners do not occur, America's transportation system will still operate. "It just won't be as efficient," he says.

Nevertheless, efficiencies in a system that costs trillions of dollars can amount to real savings, and everyone in the transportation field agrees that there are problems with efficiency.

The report lists about 80 recommendations to make the present system more efficient. These suggestions can be grouped under four themes:

—An overall reduction in federal involvement. The commission feels that the government should do less itself and restrain business less. Its conclusion: "For most transportation issues, public interest and private profit are consistent rather than opposed."

—Uniform national policy. While the same policy will

not work for each transportation issue, "policies should not work at cross-purposes," the commission says.

—Economic analysis of proposed federal actions. The government should know what a project will cost before it begins. Also, the cost benefits of alternatives should be available. Economic analysis should be applied to nontransportation goals such as environmental protection, safety, energy conservation, and national defense. For safety and research, federal involvement, including financial assistance, is required.

—Support from system users. "Free markets operate on the principle that those who benefit must pay for the costs," says the commission, which excludes urban and rural transit systems and air traffic control. These exceptions benefit the public generally, it says, and should be subsidized through taxes.

Underlying the recommendations is a complex, three-part forecast of trends and demographics that will affect transportation decisions of most businesses in the future.

The commission included low, medium, and high-growth scenarios, but generally used a medium-growth analysis. The report covers urban, rural, and intercity transportation of both freight and passengers. Its base year is 1975.

The transportation system over the next two decades shapes up like this:

—Personal travel was 2.6 trillion miles in 1975 and will grow to 4.6 trillion miles in 2000. People will depend primarily on automobiles, although airlines will carry more long-distance travelers and by 2000 burn more fuel than cars. Despite increases in mass transit, traffic jams and urban congestion will survive. Highway fatalities will increase from 46,-000 in 1975 to 67,000 in 2000, although the number of deaths per 100 million vehicle miles will go down.

—Trucks, railroads, ships, barges, and pipelines will be the freight carriers. Railroads and ships will increase their market share. Freight hauling accounted for 2.4 trillion ton-miles in 1975; by 2000, it should reach 6.3 trillion.

—America will still run predominantly on oil, although synthetic and other fuels will be used. The wellhead price of domestic crude oil, assuming deregulation, will rise 59 percent in constant dollars between 1975 and 2000. Domestic production will continue to decline until 1985 and then increase gradually. Demand will exceed domestic supply and until 1990 will be met through increased imports.

By the 1990s, synthetic crude oil will represent 20 percent of all crude oil available to refineries. Of the synthetic crude, 78 percent will be from coal.

Because of increased mining in the West, three times today's volume of coal will be moved twice its average distance, for a sixfold increase in ton-miles. The increase will mean that more energy will be spent in transporting energy.

Sufficient petroleum-based fuels can be made available for transportation only if all domestic energy resources are exploited, including solar, nuclear, oil shale, tar sands, and coal liquefaction, the commission says.

—Capital investment in transportation will equal $4.2 trillion between 1975 and 2000, with $1.2 trillion of that from various levels of government. While these are big numbers, the cost burden is actually decreasing. In 1975, the total transportation bill was 21.1 percent of gross national product. By 2000, it should decline to 19.8 percent.

In 1975, the cost of passenger transportation as a percentage of disposable income per capita was 17.6 percent. By 2000, with increases in real income, this will have dropped to 13.2 percent.

—Gross national product will be nearly $3.6 trillion in 2000, or 2.35 times 1975 GNP. There will be 260 million Americans living in 104 million households, up from 214 million Americans in 71 million households in 1975. Disposable personal income per capita will grow to $9,826, nearly double that of 1975, leaving more money available for traveling and transportation costs.

Growth Predictions

The commission predicts that average income will rise faster than the cost of owning and operating a car, that demographics will show a shift toward more and smaller households, and that the average age will continue rising, with more people reaching driving age.

In urban areas, where 75 to 80 percent of Americans live, passenger trips will grow steadily from 359.4 million in 1975 to 462.7 million in 2000. These trips account for about one third of all travel miles throughout the country.

About seven percent of the urban trips will be in mass transit vehicles, which will average about the same or slightly below the percentage in 1975. Only in cities with a million-plus people is transit ridership expected to rise.

Optimistic Estimates

One of the hazards of forecasting transportation trends shows up in the urban mass transit figures. The commission report predicts that from 1975 to 2000 bus seat-miles will grow from 232.6 million to 433.9 million. During the same time, rail (subway, light rail or trolley, and commuter rail) will grow from 172.7 million seat-miles to 437.4 million, more than doubling in 25 years.

Arthur L. Webster II, the commission's director for policy integration, says: "These estimates are probably very optimistic." Although data for the prediction were obtained in June, 1978, rail service was bullish in 1978, he says. Ridership has not kept up with seat-miles, and high expenses tend to favor expansion of bus service over subways, Mr. Webster adds.

Mass transit will play a big role during rush hours, but the dominant vehicle for urban travel will still be the passenger vehicle, whether it be a car, truck, or van. While the number of highways increases moderately, and the number of freeway lanes increases faster, there will also be a big jump in the number of urban passenger vehicles, rising from 53.8 million in 1975 to 100.1 million in 2000.

Fuel consumption in 2000, assuming greater use of diesel-powered vehicles, is expected to drop below 1975 levels.

Auto and Air Dominate

Some of the greatest changes will take place in intercity passenger movement. Measured in total passenger-miles, airlines will increase their share tremendously, bus and rail will decline from their already tiny fractions, and autos will decline slightly. Auto travel will still be nearly four times greater than air travel.

The commission report says: "While all modes exhibit absolute growth, auto and air clearly dominate, accounting for more than 97 percent of all intercity travel. The most significant shift is from auto to air, which grows at the highest rate.

"As income rises, the value of time rises, and air travel becomes more desirable because of its speed," the report adds.

Although both aircraft and cars will become more fuel efficient, planes use more energy per passenger-mile than cars. With the shift toward air travel, fuel use is expected to rise. Indeed, says the commission, "by 2000, planes may replace the auto as the dominant user of energy for intercity travel."

Interstate System

Cars today travel on 3.87 million miles of roads. Most intercity travel occurs on about 20 percent of that, and about 20 percent of all travel is on one percent of the roads, the nearly completed 42,500-mile Interstate Highway System. In 1975, autos accounted for 1,123 billion intercity passenger-miles, or about 86.3 percent of the total. In 2000, autos will account for 1,830 billion passenger-miles, or about 78.2 percent of the projected total of 2,340 billion. By 1985, smaller autos will lose ground to medium-sized autos, a trend that will continue to 2000.

However, Eugene Bordinat, Jr., vice president-design for the Ford Motor Co., believes that government regulations will force automakers to produce a lightweight, fuel-efficient city car. It won't be an electric.

Hybrid Vehicle

"I predict that the power plant of the city car will be a small, air-cooled reciprocating engine—an aluminum motorcycle engine, for example," he says. The car would carry a driver and one passenger, weigh 1,000 to 1,200 pounds, and get 50 to 60 miles per gallon.

Mr. Bordinat also sees a "practical, multipassenger, front-wheel-drive vehicle that can be readily converted into a high-volume cargo carrier, a cross between a station wagon and a van, but smaller.

"As we downsize luxury cars," he says, "we will replace pure size through the magic of electronics and new creature-comfort features—at no sacrifice to interior passenger space."

Another sort of vision came from postwar futurists who thought that by 1980 Americans would have a helicopter in every garage. Today, many Americans don't even have a garage.

The day is going to come, says Morris Belzberg, president and chief executive officer of Budget Rent-a-Car Corp., when private cars will be banned from center cities. In their place, along with mass transit, will be fleets of two-seater cars parked in strategic locations and available to anyone.

Activated by special electronics or magnetic credit cards, the autos could be driven to other sites and dropped off. A computer would keep track of how many miles a person had driven, and he would be sent a monthly bill. "Naturally," says Mr. Belzberg, "we'd like to be a part of that system."

Own Small, Rent Big

Meanwhile, Budget pushes the rental of big or special cars. "People can rent a big station wagon for the once-a-year vacation," says Mr. Belzberg, "and own a small commuter car. That's much more intelligent and prudent."

He flatly disagrees with predictions of an increase in multiple-car families and two-car families going to three cars as vehicles become more specialized. "It simply costs too much for insurance, maintenance, depreciation, and taxes," he says.

Air travel will grow from 148 billion passenger miles, or 11.4 percent of the total, to 472 billion passenger-miles, or 20.2 percent. The surge in ridership, already under way, and the ravages of inflation are hitting hard.

"We've boosted our estimate of capital needs through 1990 by 50 percent, from $60 billion to $90 billion," says George W. James, senior vice president for economics and finance at the Air Transport Association.

The commission report says "it is widely agreed that few new large airports will be built by 2000," but existing airports will be expanded. In addition, not all air travel will go to the trunk carriers. As deregulation allows the major airlines to withdraw from marginal operations, regional and commuter airlines will take over.

Every Penny Counts

"There's a trend toward more fuel-efficient planes," says Dr. James, "including the Boeing 767, 757, and 727/200, the Airbus A300, and the stretch DC-9s. Carriers are looking to a 30 to 40 percent increase in fuel efficiency."

And well they might. In the first half of 1979, jet fuel prices rose 17 cents to 58 cents a gallon. "Each penny increase costs us $115 million a year," says Dr. James. "That 17 cents translates into nearly $2 billion a year for the same amount of fuel."

Intercity buses are expected to increase their passenger-miles from 25 billion in 1975 to 31 billion in 2000, but this will be a reduction in the bus industry's percentage of the total from 1.9 to 1.3 percent.

Says the commission: "Prospects are not particularly promising for the intercity bus industry, unless fuel availabil-

ity problems induce shifts from the automobile." It adds that
bus industry productivity is limited by the 55 mph speed
limit, seating capacity of buses, and a lack of technical improvement in bus equipment.

First Class Bus Service

The intercity bus industry is more optimistic. "I foresee a
proliferation of bus service of all kinds," says Arthur D.
Lewis, president of the American Bus Association. "I think
we can expect a substantial increase not only in regular route
operations, but also in charter and tour services. Likely innovations will include first class and perhaps even higher classes
of service. Already the industry is experimenting with executive coach service seating 15 to 25 passengers in much greater
comfort."

Mr. Lewis also sees more terminals in suburbs. Lee
Whitehead, director of public relations for Greyhound Lines,
Inc., agrees. "That's where the people are," he says.

Greyhound, which accounts for 60 percent of the intercity
bus service, is pushing for total deregulation of the industry.
"Let economics, not government whim, be the deciding factor," says Mr. Whitehead. He thinks Washington is coming
around to that view.

If buses are deregulated, the discount fares used by airlines when they were deregulated will not be much use in attracting more bus riders. "Our prices are not that flexible," he
says.

Own Right of Way

Railroads accounted for five billion passenger-miles in
1975 and are expected to grow to six billion in 2000, which is
a drop in market share from 0.4 to 0.3 percent. Quasi-public,
government-sponsored Amtrak operates passenger railroads
over private, freight-hauling tracks—except in the Northeast
Corridor where it has its own right of way and 60 percent of
its ridership. Congress has allocated $1.75 billion to upgrade
the Northeast Corridor for high-speed train service.

While rail is weak in intercity passenger movement, it is and will remain the dominant freight mode in terms of ton-miles. The key to rail's strong position is coal, which the commission predicts will rise from 10.8 percent of total rail traffic in 1975 to between 14 and 20 percent by 2000. Railroads hauled 673 billion ton-miles of all freight for a 28.7 percent share of the market. By 2000, they should carry 1,983 billion ton-miles, up to 31.9 percent of the total, which is projected at 6.3 trillion ton-miles, or 2.6 times the 1975 load.

Crude Oil

Water is the only mode other than rail to show a steady increase in share of ton-miles over time, says the commission. As with rail, one commodity is critical—crude oil from Alaska. Because of Alaskan oil, water is expected to succeed pipelines in terms of ton-miles as the primary mover of crude oil by 2000. But this does not mean that oil tonnage will shift from pipelines to ships; the oil ships have long trips to make, which raises the ton-mile figure. Water transport will grow from 428 billion ton-miles in 1975 (18.3 percent of market) to 1,433 billion ton-miles (23.1 percent).

Coal accounts for 22 percent of barge traffic, a figure that will grow as more western coal is mined and transported. Federal Barge Lines, for example, is building a 15-million-ton facility to transfer coal from railcars to barges at Cora, Mo., 80 miles south of St. Louis on the Mississippi River.

John A. Creedy, president of the Water Transport Association, says that with one major exception—Lock and Dam 26 at Alton, Ill., on the Mississippi River—river system capacities far exceed today's traffic. "Of great importance," he says, "is increased coordination between rail and water modes, a continuation of the trend that has been going on quietly for years." Mr. Creedy suggests that railroads, many of which run east-west, can increase profits by greater coordination with barge lines on the Mississippi.

Urban freight movement, the commission notes, is an area in which "little success has been achieved in collecting data." Nevertheless, the trend is toward more frequent deliveries of smaller shipments. The number of truck-miles will increase faster than the number of trucks, reflecting a change in distribution patterns as more truck terminals move out of the central business districts into the suburbs with good access to freeway interchanges. One problem: More delivery trucks on the urban streets will cause more congestion and air pollution.

While both common carrier and private trucking will grow, its share of the market will remain about the same. Again, this is predicted on rail and water carrying the commodities with the highest growth. Intercity trucks accounted for 488 billion ton-miles in 1975 for a 20.8 percent share of the market. By 2000, they will be up to 1,366 billion ton-miles for a 22 percent share.

Pipelines Lose Share

Pipelines, both oil and gas, are expected to lose market share by the end of the century. Oil pipelines will grow in absolute terms from 437 billion ton-miles, to 1,062 billion ton-miles, but market share will drop from 18.6 to 17.1 percent. Gas pipelines will grow from 312 billion ton-miles to 356 billion ton-miles, with market share dropping from 13.3 to 5.7 percent.

Air freight's share of the market remains constant at 0.2 percent. In absolute terms air freight will grow from four billion to ten billion ton-miles.

Looking at the commission's overall forecasts, Senator Russell B. Long (D.-La.), a commission member, says:

Two overriding themes emerge. First, our transportation system structure must be upgraded and maintained to enable it to move the domestic energy required to meet our future needs. This will require substantial funding.

Second, we must strongly develop domestic fuels for transportation, which are vital for economic survival. This means increased domestic production of crude oil and rigorous development of alternative petroleum-based sources such as coal and shale oil and renewable liquid fuels such as alcohols from biomass, solid waste, and coal.

Looking at the challenges over the next 20 years, Mr. Belzberg of Budget Rent-a-Car says the nation cannot wait that long. He calls for a major project like the one that produced the atom bomb to upgrade and expand the nation's transportation system and develop energy self-sufficiency.

"If we have to wait 20 years," he says, "this country will be owned by the Arabs."

TRANSPORTATION: THE ROADS (AND BUSES AND TRAINS) FROM HERE[5]

There is one basic fact that anyone should know about transportation systems in the United States, and that is that they are falling apart. Almost three decades of building roads and bridges, coupled with drastic losses in mass transit ridership, allowed us to ignore one question: how were we going to maintain and replace those roads and bridges, those massive public works investments? We could build them because revenues were increasing faster than costs and because there seemed to be a limitless demand for new construction. We are now in a decade of both declining revenues and declining expectations.

The transportation question of the '80s is how much to spend for new construction and equipment, compared to the amount we spend to maintain and replace those previously invested in.

The Council of State Planning Agencies documented the current extent of neglect in its book *America in Ruins*. It says the interstate highway system "is deteriorating at a rate requiring reconstruction of 2000 miles of road per year." According to the report, reconstructing roads and bridges will probably cost more than $250 billion during the 1980s. On the transit side, bus fleets are not being replaced at a reason-

[5] Reprint of article by Tom Downs, director, Dept. of Transportation, District of Columbia and Neil Goldstein, Sierra Club's New York representative. *Sierra*. 67:26+. Mr./Ap. '82. Reprinted with permission from Sierra, The Sierra Club Bulletin. © 1982 by the Sierra Club.

able rate, many maintenance facilities are falling down, and some of our rail systems are in the worst shape of any in the world.

This debate over what type of investment is best for transit and highways is not an academic exercise. In recent years both Boston and Chicago shut down their rail systems temporarily, each when the money had run out. Both managed to get emergency appropriations from their state legislatures to keep going, but their long-term financial futures continue to look dim, and in both cities the transit systems as a whole are financial basket cases. In Birmingham, Alabama, the transit system closed entirely for an extended period of time, and when it reopened, it had reduced its fleet and routes considerably.

Clearly, unless revenues are increased there will be insufficient funds in the Highway Trust Fund both to build new highways and to rehabilitate existing roads. In its drive to reduce the burden on the federal taxpayer, the administration also has indicated its desire to reduce federal assistance from general tax revenues for mass transit. Together, these factors pose a serious dilemma for the administration's transportation policymakers concerned about the decayed state of our transportation system. So serious was this concern that Transportation Secretary Drew Lewis explored a proposal to add five cents per gallon to gasoline taxes to raise revenues. (The current tax is four cents per gallon; it has not changed in 20 years.) Each cent of gasoline tax is worth approximately $1.1 billion in total revenues, so the proposal, had it been accepted by President Reagan and Congress, could have raised an additional $5.5 billion for transportation rehabilitation and construction.

In addition to revenue shortages creating pressure for reanalysis of transportation priorities, the legislative process creates more pressures of its own. The legislative authorization of both the mass transit program and the highway program expire in 1982. New national legislation will have to be passed defining the future direction and size of the programs. The administration plans to make significant changes in both programs. Last year the administration and Congress redefined allowable costs for highway construction; they also reduced the total size of the proposed interstate highway system. But the approved "no frills" highway bill did not incorporate the administration's proposal to eliminate aid for urban systems and rural roads. Nor has Congress accepted the administration's proposal to eliminate federal operating assistance for public transit.

Previous experience indicates that the new legislation will be a combined bill covering both transit and highways. In the House of Representatives this arrangement makes sense, since the Public Works Committee has jurisdiction over both highway and transit legislation. But in the Senate, jurisdiction is divided; the Environment and Public Works Committee has the highway program, and the Banking Committee has the transit program.

Currently the highway program is financed by a trust fund established in 1956 to provide a system of highways to improve our national defense. The fund is generated by the previously mentioned four-cent-per-gallon gas tax. The tax is categorized as a user charge, providing the traditional legislative rationale to retain the fund—the users pay for the facilities. The major highway programs and their funding levels for fiscal year 1982 (the current year) are:

Interstate highway construction: This is the program that funds major construction on this road system. Its 1982 appropriation level is $3.1 billion.

Interstate reconstruction (called 4R): This fund allows states to rebuild and repair existing interstate highways. It is allocated $800 million for 1982.

Primary roads: This is also a major construction fund for the old U.S. highway system's numbered routes. It is funded at $1.5 billion for 1982.

Secondary roads: Generally speaking, these funds are for major country roads. The allocation is $400 million for 1982.

Urban roads: This program funds major urban streets and can also be used for transit projects. Its appropriation is $800 million for 1982.

Bridges: The bridge program provides funds for reconstructing bridges, both on and off the federal system. It is allocated $900 million for 1982.

The total spending authority for the highway program is $8 billion for fiscal 1982. But the fund's revenues are now at least a billion dollars a year below expenditures, so the fund is drawing on its reserves; the current balance is about $9 billion.

The most controversial highway program by far is the interstate construction program. The most controversial, expensive and environmentally damaging projects have been postponed to the very end; some are still to come. They carry enormous price tags and drain funds from areas that desperately need to reconstruct crumbling roads and bridges. Some of these projects, such as I-478 in New York (known as Westway) and I-105 in Los Angeles (known as the Century Freeway addition), have enormous price tags and are being criticized by other states that have to be content with less funding for reconstruction while these projects use scarce dollars.

Environmentalists have also criticized these projects for using money that could be spent on mass transit projects. When a state decides to forego a previously planned segment of the interstate highway system, the funds allocated to the project are turned into an entitlement for the state that can be used to assist mass transit. To show how expensive these projects are, the combined cost of Westway and the Century addition is more than $4 billion for 21.5 miles of roadway.

To eliminate some costs in the interstate construction program, in the fall of 1981 Congress limited the types of projects that could be built with interstate construction funds; but these large-scale projects still receive priority funding because they are classified as "gaps" in the interstate highway system.

If the picture for highways is dim, however, the picture for mass transit is dark. In fiscal 1981, the Urban Mass Transit Administration had authority to spend $4.6 billion on transit nationwide. In fiscal 1982, the program will be funded at $3.7 billion. This is a reduction of almost 20%.

The transit-funding program has two major components, capital development and operating assistance. The capital development program provides federal funding for 80% of a local program, with the other 20% coming from the locality, to purchase new buses, bus garages or rail transit facilities. The operating assistance program helps transit systems meet operating costs while keeping fares low to encourage ridership. The Reagan administration's position is that the operating assistance program is not effective, so this program will be phased out over the next three years. This phaseout would reduce the funds by a third each year and would terminate the program at the end of the third year. Currently one billion dollars a year in federal operating assistance go to transit systems, so the impact of eliminating this program would be to reduce funding by another billion dollars; that is, the annual funding level would be about $2.7 billion dollars a year for transit, if nothing else changed. The transit program would be cut in half, a disaster for the transit systems of the nation.

The cut would come in hard times. Transit ridership has decreased again because of escalating fares and minor reductions in gasoline prices. In October 1981, transit ridership nationally was down 7.3% compared to the same period in 1980, a sign that transit continues to need assistance, not starvation, from the federal government.

The issues raised by the administration's legislative proposals and the President's rejection of Secretary Lewis's proposed increases in gasoline and excise tax revenues continued to confront Congress and transportation policy makers. First, the federal highway program currently spends $1.5 billion per year more than it takes in because gasoline consumption is down nationwide. To make matters worse, in addition to the substantial costs of new highway construction borne by the Highway Trust Fund, many interstate highways are now approaching their 30-year design lifetimes. While past programs of resurfacing, restoration and rehabilitation have maintained roadways during their design lifetimes, ordinary maintenance measures can no longer suffice; reconstruction work in many cases will be required. This expansion of the program by increasing funding will add many billions of dollars of costs when revenues can't even pay for the current program.

While this revenue shortage poses a dilemma, the Sierra Club's transportation activists have seized upon it as an opportunity to encourage a reevaluation of highway spending. As an alternative to spending limited funds on the new construction, Club leaders have proposed a reduction in highway spending for such projects and a redirection of funds to an expanded reconstruction program. In meetings with Transportation Secretary Drew Lewis and Federal Highway Administrator Barnhart, in congressional testimony and in discussions with local government officials, Club representatives have urged this change in policy.

A second major transportation issue also concerns financing. Currently trucks cause a disproportionate amount of highway damage. As a vehicle's weight doubles, highway wear and tear increases eightfold. Since the administration has rejected tax increases, it would appear sensible therefore to redistribute the existing tax burden so trucks pay their fair share. The American Association of Railroads, the Sierra Club, the National Wildlife Federation, the Environmental Policy Center and many other groups have spoken out forcefully in favor of this equity. Moreover [Mr. Goldstein notes], the subsidy that auto drivers provide to trucks by paying a disproportionate share of gasoline taxes to support highways has important environmental consequences: subsidizing trucks encourages using trucks instead of more energy-efficient and less-polluting rail freight systems.

The administration's proposals to eliminate urban and rural aid raise another issue of fairness. Currently, mile for mile, rural roads and local city streets are used far more than interstate highways. But most gasoline taxes derived from this ridership pay for the interstate system. The result of this subsidy of interstate highways [Mr. Goldstein points out] is the construction of environmentally damaging new interstate roadways. Rather than reduced aid to urban systems or rural roads, environmentalists have urged that money be redirected from the interstate system back to localities.

Transit systems are going to face a very traumatic future, with the phaseout of operating assistance, increasing fares and declining ridership. Transit almost died out in the United States before we discovered that we had to have it. Mass transit now needs not only a financial and philosophical commitment from the federal government, but also greater flexibility for local governments and agencies to use in allocating funds. In the past, for example, local officials have been restricted from applying funds to some kinds of transit systems, thus limiting their choices. In addition, operating-assistance funds have been disbursed according to fixed formulas, leaving big systems with few dollars per rider and small systems with more per rider. But needs vary from system to system, and local officials should have more flexibility in allocating funds according to what their systems need.

The administration's proposals raise serious issues regarding starting new rail projects, too. In the budget documents justifying its freeze on such projects, the administration argued that mass transit systems save little energy in the short run, when the energy needed for construction is considered. This analysis may be in error because it relies on studies that do not fully consider the energy required to build the alternative, highways for cars; but it *certainly* misses the essential point named by mass-transit advocates regarding the energy and environmental advantages of transit. When mass transit systems are planned in conjunction with other sensible urban-development policies and land-use (zoning) practices, and when the most appropriate system is chosen for the circumstances (light rail where it makes sense, heavy rail where that is justified, buses where they work best, and so on), mass transit systems are important factors in encouraging compact development.

Mass transit encourages compact development. It can reduce people's need to make trips in *any* vehicle, since people in cities with mass transit systems can walk rather than drive, as they must do in sprawling, auto-dependent developments.

It can mean that energy efficient high-density housing could be built rather than less efficient low-density residences. Of course, mass transit also pollutes less than massive use of individual cars.

In summary, the highway and mass transit programs both suffer from years of neglect of existing facilities and equipment. As a nation we have yet to demonstrate that we are able and willing to maintain what we have already built. Until we do, there is little reason continually to expand. Rehabilitating existing systems uses fewer resources per dollar than new construction. The new authorization for the highway and transit programs should direct more money to maintenance and reconstruction before expanding the systems.

Also, the administration's proposals for transportation systems do not handle the crisis of decaying and financially distressed systems in many major cities. Nor do these proposals appear to satisfy the nation's energy needs. These are matters that must be clearly dealt with in this year's legislative proposals for transportation. These issues are essential items for this year's congressional consideration of transportation; the results of the debate may establish the direction transportation systems will go for decades.

PUBLIC ENTERPRISE AND PUBLIC TRANSPORTATION[6]

For the nation's mass transit industry, the news this year could hardly have been more depressing. First came a White House announcement that federal operating subsidies were to be phased out by 1985 and capital assistance seriously curtailed. Then, adding insult to injury, came a report from the General Accounting Office criticizing transit's inability to control operating costs and warning that the growing demand

[6] Reprint of article by C. Kenneth Orski, vice president, German Marshall Fund of the US. *USA Today.* 110:54–6. N. '81. Copyright 1981 by the Society for the Advancement of Education. Reprinted by permission.

for subsidies was approaching "crisis proportions." Finally, as if to seal the verdict, a new Census Bureau report revealed that, despite rising gasoline prices, the percentage of commuters using public transit declined during the 1970s. Cast over it all has been a climate of growing public disenchantment with transit's performance, a sense that six years of federal operating subsidies have done little to improve the quality of public transportation.

A combination of spiralling labor costs, unrealistically low fares, deferred maintenance, and low labor productivity have pushed transit operating deficits to record heights. They were $2,000,000,000 in 1978, climbed to $2,700,000,000 in 1979, and reached a staggering $3,200,000,000 in 1980. If this trend continues unchecked, transit deficits could exceed $6,000,-000,000 by 1985. Only federal subsidies, currently covering about one-third of total deficits, have saved many systems from financial collapse. Eliminating these subsidies, warn local officials, would deal a death blow to public transportation.

Is this apocalyptic view of transit's future justified? Are federal subsidies really that essential to transit's survival? Or have they, on the contrary, done the public a disservice by masking transit's underlying weaknesses and postponing necessary and long-overdue reforms that would render public transportation once again economically viable?

Certainly, any cutbacks in federal assistance will intensify pressures on the already financially strapped local governments. Many cities, locked into labor contracts with automatic cost-of-living escalator clauses, will have no alternative but to raise fares in order to compensate for the loss of federal subsidies. Higher fares would not necessarily be out of order, having generally lagged far behind inflation. Between 1972 and 1978, for example, the average fare adjusted for inflation actually *decreased* by 16.7 percent. Raising fares would merely help to restore a more realistic and equitable relationship between passenger fare revenues and public subsidies than today's typical two-to-three fare-to-subsidy ratio.

Would higher fares depress transit ridership? This is not

necessarily true, especially since automobile costs also keep rising. In 1980, the cost of auto operation increased by 20 percent to an average of 42 cents per mile. The average transit fare, on the other hand, was still only 43 cents in late 1980, although many cities had raised them during the year. Thus, fares for commuters could be raised substantially—perhaps as high as $1—without rendering mass transportation uncompetitive with driving an automobile.

Fare hikes alone, however, can not solve transit's fiscal problems. Even if fares did rise to $1, the additional revenue generated quickly would be gobbled up by new increases in operating costs. Transit's running costs have grown explosively in recent years—from $2,500,000,000 in 1973 to $6,-000,000,000 in 1980—and they show no evidence of subsiding. Contributing to the cost escalation is a set of factors that include soaring fuels costs (although these account for the smallest component of the escalation), liberal wage settlements that are often inflated by compulsory binding arbitration requirements, frequent automatic cost-of-living wage adjustments, and service expansion into outlying low-density suburbs far beyond transit's traditional markets. Compounding the problem are workrules that prohibit split shifts (i.e., unpaid breaks during daytime hours, when demand for transit falls off) and labor contracts barring the hiring of part-time drivers, both of which keep transit productivity from rising.

With fare boosts unable to fully compensate for skyrocketing operating costs, local and state governments will be forced to look for new sources of revenue to make up for the lost federal subsidies. However, given the current climate of fiscal conservatism, local jurisdictions are not likely to find much public support for new transit-related taxes. Instead, transit authorities may be forced to cut service and eliminate marginal lines. Most vulnerable will be chronically underused and unprofitable suburban bus routes which mushroomed during the 1970s, largely because of generous federal subsidies. These routes, in low-density areas beyond transit's traditional markets, will increasingly come to be considered as an expendable luxury by transit officials looking desperately for ways to reduce operating costs.

The pressure to drop suburban services will also stem from suburban jurisdictions themselves, as local officials come to realize that they can save money by breaking off from costly metropolitan-wide transit systems and providing transit services of their own, either running the buses themselves or contracting for services with private bus and taxi operators. One forerunner of this trend is Montgomery County in suburban Washington, D.C., which has operated a local bus system for the past five years. Today, the 155-bus Ride-On system carries 20,000 passengers a day, is growing at a rate of 10 percent per year—and operates without a cent of federal subsidy.

There is a solid economic rationale behind Montgomery County's decision to replace the Metropolitan Transit Authority's buses with their own. Ride-On pays its drivers $5-6,-000 less than the Transit Authority; uses as many part-time and substitute drivers as it wants; operates smaller, less expensive buses; and has a leaner administrative organization. The resulting savings translate into significantly lower operating costs. In 1980, it cost the county $20 per hour to operate Ride-On and $37 per hour to purchase bus service from the Transit Authority. Looking at it another way, it costs 80 cents to carry a passenger on the local system and 95 cents on one of the Transit Authority buses. Faced with an imminent increase in its annual contribution to the regional system, it is little wonder that the county is expanding its fleet of vehicles with a view to replacing additional Transit Authority services. Other Washington suburban jurisdictions contemplate parallel moves.

Similar efforts to decentralize transportation service delivery are taking place elsewhere in the country. In the Chicago area, for example, the Regional Transportation Authority serves as a funding and coordinating body, but leaves the management and operating responsibilities in the hands of local jurisdictions. Local communities, in turn, contract with private operators to provide needed services.

Some local officials view the prospect of independent sub-urban services with considerable alarm, as a prelude to an eventual "balkanization" of the carefully assembled metropolitan transportation systems. They perceive the efforts of suburban jurisdictions to break away from areawide systems as a subversion of the cherished and carefully nurtured principle of regional cooperation which has been viewed as a cornerstone of any progress toward metropolitan government.

These sentiments, however, betray a certain confusion about the aims of centralization. No doubt, schedule- and fare-setting properly belong in a metropolitan-level agency, for coordinated timetables and uniform fares are essential to the concept of a unified, areawide transportation system, but does the same reasoning apply to transit *operation*? Is centralized management necessary to efficient delivery of transit services? One has reason to doubt it. Indeed, all evidence points in the opposite direction: decentralized, locally run systems seem to function more efficiently and deliver service at lower cost than centrally managed systems run by metropolitan transit authorities. Moreover, small community-managed systems are likely to be more politically accountable and allow citizens to exercise a greater measure of control over costs and quality of service than regional public bodies, which are controlled by governing boards made up of appointed officials and operate in an environment insulated from public oversight.

A Creative Approach

Once we discard the notion that provision of transit service must remain the exclusive province of area-wide public monopolies, we can begin thinking in more creative terms. We can imagine a transportation system that provides different service to different client groups and tailors service closely to the needs of each client.

Such a decentralized and diversified transit system would rely heavily on the private sector for financial support. Business has a strong incentive to help preserve public transportation. It is, after all, one of its principal beneficiaries. Employers benefit from good public transportation by gaining access to an expanded labor pool. Merchants and shopping centers profit by reaching more potential customers. Developers gain from improved transportation access by having a greater choice of sites to build on and by having their land holdings increase in value. Each group has an enormous financial stake in maintaining efficient local transportation, and each should be expected to share in the cost of providing it to the public.

Private enterprise also has a right to demand a greater role in the *operation* of transportation services. Private operators are generally more cost-conscious, consumer-oriented, and innovative than public transit authorities, which operate as areawide monopolies, with many of the inefficiencies of large bureaucracies. In suburbs and in smaller cities, especially, locally based private transportation firms might often be able to provide better, more flexible, and more cost-effective service than public transit agencies.

Having abandoned the confining belief that tax-supported public agencies must be the sole providers of transportation services, we can envision a panoply of specialized transportation services, tailored to the demands of particular markets. A few examples will suffice:

—Express bus services, offered on a subscription basis by private charter bus operators, that would carry commuters from suburban locations to downtown destinations and from central cities to major suburban employment centers. Such private "buspools" already operate without subsidies in some communities—for example, Columbia, Md.; Lexington, Mass.; St. Louis; New York City; and Southern California—at costs far below those of regular transit service.

—Shared-taxi services, furnished by private taxi operators, that would substitute for regular bus service along certain routes in off-peak hours, at night, and on weekends, when transit demand falls off to a level that is too low to justify running full-size buses. Substitute taxi service has been introduced successfully in Phoenix, Ariz., and in certain German cities, where it is producing large savings to the taxpayers.

—Employer-provided transportation to work, in the form of company-organized vanpools and carpools and company-owned and -operated buses. Employer-furnished transportation and employer-provided travel allowances have long been a standard provision of labor contracts in Europe. There is still a vast potential to expand employer-sponsored transportation to work in cities large and small.

—Community-sponsored minibus and van fleets, operated under contract by private entrepreneurs, that would provide local daytime circulation service within suburban communities and collection/distribution service for commuters using linehaul buses and trains. Such community-based transit systems already operate successfully in a number of suburban locations—e.g., in Montgomery County, Md., and in Chicago suburbs.

—Privately funded and operated shuttle systems that would link suburban centers and linehaul transportation systems with regional shopping malls, industrial parks, and major suburban employment centers, as well as with outlying residential developments. The cost of operating such services could be internalized, much in the same vein as the cost of elevators and escalators within buildings.

—Privately funded and operated bus lines that would serve outlying resorts, amusement parks, and other private recreational facilities. Such services could be set up permanently to attract carless persons or on a stand-by basis to be activated in times of emergency fuel shortages.

—Neighborhood-based networks of private automobile leasing and rental agencies that would provide urban residents with efficient and inexpensive "public automobile" service. This could include provision of specialized vehicles that are needed only occasionally (e.g., station wagons, pick-up trucks, recreational vehicles, etc.) as well as short-term rentals.

—Special on-call transportation services for elderly and handicapped persons; run by voluntary and social service organizations or operated under contract by local taxi companies, that would replace the present expensive regulatory approach requiring cities to furnish "fully accessible" buses.

—Rural transportation services that would combine postal service, package delivery, school transportation, and passenger services. Such combined services have been operating successfully in Europe and may be the most efficient way to provide public transportation service in sparsely populated rural areas.

To achieve this more pluralistic approach to transportation, the federal government would have to relax the regulatory noose it has tied around transit and provide incentives to encourage greater private sector participation in the provision of mass transportation. A key first step would be to modify the operation of labor protection provisions so as to allow development of innovative transportation services. Another important move would be to work toward elimination of legal impediments and other barriers, such as restrictive insurance regulations, that inhibit introduction and operation of nontraditional transportation services—*e.g.*, subscription buses and jitneys.

At the same time, we need a program of positive incentives. These could take the form of tax credits to private employers who sponsor employee transportation and favorable tax treatment of innovative, privately operated mass transportation services, substituted in place of publicly funded mass transit.

Above all, we need a change in perspective—a new vision that recognizes provision of transportation as a joint responsibility of the public and private sectors, and that regards a pluralistic approach and competition in service delivery as essential conditions to restoring vitality to urban transportation.

II. AN ENVIRONMENTAL SOLUTION—RAILROADS

EDITOR'S INTRODUCTION

"The true history of the United States is the history of transportation . . . in which the names of railroad presidents are more significant than those of Presidents of the United States," noted the historian Philip Guedalla. While his colleagues may quarrel about this observation, few historians would question the impact of railroads on the history, the economy, and even the culture of America. This section surveys the current situation of America's railroads, now suffering from over-regulation, financial problems, and a reduced number of passengers.

The group of articles entitled "Railroads: Their Impact on Business in the Coming Decade," by William H. Jones and reprinted from *Dun's Review,* provides an economic overview of the railroad industry and foresees a generally bright future for passenger and freight transportation, albeit with some problems. Some of these problems are spelled out in the second article in the section, as Graham Beene finds Amtrak beset by troubles and more troubles. His essay, reprinted from *Washington Monthly,* poses the problem succinctly, "Where Are You, Benito, Now That We Need You?" The next excerpt, from an article in *Forbes,* describes some effects of the Staggers Rail Act and government deregulation on American railroads.

Finally on an optimistic note, Professor Foegen of Winona State College, writing in the *Futurist,* foresees high-speed and comfortable trains, like those developed in foreign countries, that will once again attract the American traveler in large numbers, as in the past.

LESS BUMPY TRACK SEEN FOR THE 80s[1]

America's railroads have been an integral part of the national economy for over a century.

However, the railroad industry is particularly sensitive to business cycles. Every recession has impacted an industry with immense fixed plant and equipment costs, and railroad history as a result includes many chapters of bankruptcy.

Congress has been forced to respond to the changing economic forces that have affected railroading, with major legislation in 1850, 1867, 1887, 1893, 1903, 1913, 1920, 1926, 1933, 1940 and 1958. By itself, this list underscores the importance of railroads to our economic health.

But in recent years, the governmental focus on railroad problems has accelerated. Major legislation was passed in 1970, 1973 and 1976—and still the industry's problems seem to grow. This perception stems from the greatest failure in American business history—the collapse of the merged New York Central and Pennsylvania railroad empires in mid-1970, little more than two years after a consolidation supposed to preserve private enterprise rail transportation in the densely populated Northeast.

In quick succession, half a dozen smaller rail companies failed. The question of survival was not confined to the Northeast. Indeed, as the 1980s opened, it seemed certain that two of the great Midwest-based railroads also were about to cease operations.

The failure of some of the proudest names in railroading, the prospects for mild recession in 1980 and slow long-term economic growth, a record of declining intercity freight market share, continued low return on investment and capital requirements of up to $16 billion through 1985—all combine to make it easy (and in some quarters, fashionable) to paint a bleak portrait of the industry's future.

---

[1] Articles, entitled "Railroads: Their Impact on Business in the Coming Decade," by William H. Jones. *Dun's Review.* Ap. '80. p 28–38. "Reprinted with the special permission of Dun's Review. Copyright 1980, Dun & Bradstreet Publications Corporation."

However, this does not reflect accurately the railroad industry or its impact on American business.

Over the last two decades, when every American institution was under attack, there emerged a degree of optimism within the railroad industry that the next decade will provide an opportunity for the establishment of public policies under which the railroads will prosper.

Behind this optimism are many factors, including the introduction of new technologies and computer systems as well as an infusion of young management talent at the railroads.

But two developments are paramount. For one, the American public is fed up with big government. In earlier decades, suggesting nationalization to maintain a vital national service might have been acceptable, but not so today. Second—and most important—is awareness of limited energy resources.

The railroad industry should be a major beneficiary of these two developments. Because of perennial burdens under government regulation and the likelihood that continued federal control over every little management decision is doing nothing to halt the erosion of a vital transportation network, it is likely that ICC regulation finally will be reduced.

And, because of relative railroad energy efficiency coupled with the industry's role as a transporter of coal when that commodity is being favored as an alternative to oil, there is a consensus that rail volume in the 1980s can only increase.

Historians may record that nationalization of this country's railroad system, which appeared certain in the decade of the 1970s, was only narrowly averted.

Louis W. Menk, chairman of the board of Burlington Northern Inc., agrees. Complex national industries, such as the railroad network, "don't disappear suddenly like exploding stars," he explains. "They sicken and shrivel and fade into history. . . . Until the energy shortages of the 1970s snapped them awake, American voters were allowing the regulators to push the American railroads slowly toward nationalization. . . . the last stop on the way to the museum."

In Menk's view, without the competitive market system,

government-appointed railroad managers would run up such huge deficits so Congress would be "forced to trim the national railroad system to the bone until the only freight would be the stuff they couldn't fit into a truck or a plane or a pipeline."

However, painful choices still must be made and the price for retaining a vital, nongovernmental transportation link will be increased revenues to make the business profitable enough to maintain and expand its facilities.

"It is just perfectly obvious that the overall problems of the industry are largely financial in nature," says Benjamin F. Biaggini, chairman of the board of Southern Pacific Co.

"Railroads individually, and as a group, have for many years consistently suffered inadequate rates of return, and today this results in tremendous problems in attracting capital at affordable cost. Key government leaders are acknowledging this and recently have recognized that we have reached the absolute point of choice between either letting the railroads earn a fair return or else putting the whole country on notice that it must be prepared to pay the staggering bill . . . for the preservation of those routes absolutely essential to the economy," Biaggini said in a Washington address last year.

One of those government leaders is President Carter, who support[ed] reduced federal controls over railroad industry decision-making. In his 1980 State of the Union message, the President described the railroads as "traditionally . . . one of the most overregulated industries in America."

Because of the government, President Carter said, "management initiative, service and competitive pricing have been stifled." He said railroad facilities had deteriorated, that the average rail industry return on investment is "far too low," and he emphasized that enactment of proposed rail deregulation in 1980 "is essential to restoring our railroad system to its former strength."

As important as the regulatory question is to the railroad industry (where the term "re-regulation" is preferred in contrast to the politicians' "de-regulation"), there is no unanimity about all of the ramifications of a reduced federal role.

Many railroad executives doubt any substantive changes. They see salvation for their business through initiatives that they can attempt under the current regulatory framework—mergers; increased promotion of intermodal "piggyback" traffic (trucks and trailers or containers on flatcars); promotion of energy efficiency; experiments with freight rate structures permitted by legislation of the 1970s; new services tailored to commodity shipping needs such as high-speed unit trains; aggressive marketing of factory and distribution sites along railroad rights-of-way and continued investment of available capital in new equipment and improved facilities.

Norfolk & Western Railway Co. Chairman John P. Fishwick is convinced that the proposals for reducing government regulation are premature. Within the industry, Fishwick often takes a maverick stand on railroad problems, but he heads a rail company that is one of the most profitable and most successful.

He finds no industry disagreement when he argues that railroads have inadequate earnings and cash flow and that "unless this problem is solved, the railroads cannot long continue to operate without continuous funding by government or government ownership."

Fishwick also finds some regulatory reform desirable, but he believes that deregulation will not add enough revenues, curb enough costs or facilitate enough restructuring to make the industry healthy.

What would happen with deregulation, he argues, is that it would only amount to a redistribution of existing revenues within the industry—with small railroads losing revenues to the giants who have the most to gain from carrying as much as possible of their own shipments. More sick firms would be created and that would hamper orderly mergers into the viable system that is necessary, Fishwick prophesies.

Since the early days of the industry, there have been mergers. Each economic recession has spawned a new wave of consolidation. In fact, the Norfolk & Western itself is the product of a series of mergers during a period when the

Chessie System, Inc. and the Burlington Northern were being formed.

But the debacle of the Penn Central ended merger talk for a while because it raised questions about the feasibility of combining large railroads into a single giant.

However, the Burlington Northern has not repeated the mistakes of the Penn Central and has become one of the stronger railroads. With some encouragement given to rail mergers in the legislation of the 1970s—including a limitation on ICC hearings that took over a decade to complete in the Union Pacific's proposed takeover of the Rock Island—a new wave of important mergers has surfaced, and industry consolidation will be a major trend in the 1980s.

If consolidations take place, further merger proposals can be expected. Indeed, railroad industry unity on common problems may be difficult to achieve because companies affected by proposed mergers traditionally take part in ICC proceedings and seek benefits such as trackage rights or sale of a particular line as a condition to government approval.

James G. Shea, vice president for public relations of Southern Pacific, observes that a "lack of cohesiveness" may be the industry's greatest problem, which recalls the Joseph Eastman warning in 1934 that the industry must work collectively to operate what essentially is a national asset—a railroad system divided into many parts of separate ownership.

Adds Southern Railway System Chairman Stanley Crane: "We must tell the general public where we want to go and why. Cohesiveness is a great strength . . . but we must make our voices heard in the political and economic arenas. The railroads are the most efficient in energy, the prime haulers of coal and not irrevocably linked to oil as fuel. The recipe for a strong railroad must be understood as widely as possible."

Crane's recipe includes a number of ingredients, such as more freedom for railroad management decisions on pricing and services, "assessing demand and not petitioning the government to act."

Ultimately, Crane wants to add some common ownership of railroads and trucking to provide combined short-haul and long-haul transportation; some railroad companies already operate trucking subsidiaries, having owned them before federal laws against such acquisitions.

"I do not have to tell you how much the world has changed since that concept became part of our transportation law and regulation many decades ago. Today, a truck line or barge line would be just as likely as a railroad to have the financial strength to become the core of a multimodal transportation company. But the barriers still stand," he says.

As Crane describes the current situation, management limited to one mode of transportation will try to get as much traffic for as long a haul as is possible "whether or not that is the most effective way to handle a particular transportation requirement."

The challenge of the 1980s, according to the Southern chief, will be to "get freight to the receiver's loading platform—as rapidly, as reliably, as economically and with as sparing use of fuel as we can manage." This cannot happen with present government rules preserving rigid separation of transportation modes while future needs "seem inevitably to draw various single modes into close relationships," he states.

The final strong ingredient in Crane's recipe is improved service. But, he argues, profitability must be increased to provide the resources for improved freight service.

As Burlington Northern's Menk has noted, he hasn't "seen a study, either private or government-sponsored, that doesn't forecast significant increases in freight traffic." A National Transportation Policy Study Commission report predicts that railroads could increase their ton-mile volume about 51 percent by the mid-1980s and double traffic by the end of the decade.

John V. Pincavage Jr., vice president and senior transportation analyst at Paine Webber, Mitchell Hutchins, thinks the 1980s are going to be "an extremely attractive period for railroads generally. . . . Shippers are having to rethink their entire distribution systems, which basically were designed for 12 cents a gallon diesel fuel."

Burned by inaccurate economic forecasts in recent years,

few persons today want to predict much about the future shape of business for 1980 and beyond.

Nevertheless, it is certain that America will start to elect energy-efficiency where possible. Transportation, which overall accounts for about 22 cents of each dollar of Gross National Product, also consumes more than half of all the petroleum used in the United States. For long distances, in particular, the railroads consume less energy than shipment by trucks over the highway system.

In this environment, some freight probably will shift to the railroads. Much of the added tonnage may be in intermodal, truck-rail services that already exist or will be developed by cooperative ventures between truckers and the railroad industry.

The new emphasis on railroad freight will force the industry to be reshaped, through mergers or agreements for joint use of facilities. Marketing to meet special custom needs will increase.

But will the railroads be modernized and financed to handle this task? Will government policy be altered enough to establish initiative and decision-making in the industry and away from Washington?

Most railroad executives are more optimistic than at any time during the past two decades.

As former Secretary of Transportation William T. Coleman Jr., says: "With our railroads, we no longer have any margin for error."

OVERVIEW

The nation's total freight bill each year is now about $200 billion, of which more than $23 billion goes to the major railroads.

The revenues received by the railroads pay for moving more than one-third of intercity freight, the largest single share of freight tonnage moved by any of the various modes of transportation. The rails haul 77 percent of pulp and paper shipments, 73 percent of automotive parts, 70 percent of coal and 60 percent of the grain shipped.

Intercity truckers and local truckers account for some three-quarters of the annual freight bill and trucks carry about one-fourth of all intercity freight. The balance of freight ton miles and revenues are divided between water carriers, pipelines and airlines.

However, according to Transportation Association of America figures, the railroads in 1977 (the last year for which figures are available) burned 93.8 million barrels of fuel, or just 2.75 percent of total national consumption. At the same time, trucks used 903.9 million barrels—26.49 percent of the national total. Tractor-trailer combinations used 2.78 percent and single trucks used 18.3 percent.

It is clear that the trucking business uses a lot more fuel than do the railroads—about ten times as much overall. Even if local trucking is ignored (in 1978, intercity freight truck revenues were $79.5 billion compared with $67.6 billion for local trucking), it is evident that the railroads are moving more freight than trucks and burning less fuel.

For this reason alone, there is a consensus within the railroad industry that its destiny in the 1980s is to carry an increasing share of the nation's intercity freight tonnage—ending a decline since World War II that has seen the rails' share slip sharply from close to 60 percent to under 40 percent, while energy was relatively cheap.

Last year may have been the turning point, although final tonnage figures aren't yet available for all types of intercity transportation. Even so, it is clear that new awareness of energy costs and potential oil shortages can only benefit the railroad industry.

It's true that the relative energy efficiency of the nation's interstate pipeline system and waterways—for the liquid and bulk commodities these modes carry—means that their share of intercity business also should increase. And modern trucking fleets will be required for local and short-haul business.

The number of railroads will be reduced in the 1980s

through merger and consolidation, and ultimate survival in the private sector will require rail corporations to be more conscious of service requirements for their current and new customers.

Industry executives appear to be committed to providing such attention. Moreover, record capital spending plans to improve facilities have been announced by most of the major railroads even though the national economy is in an era of slow growth that approaches recession.

"The industry will have in 1980 an opportunity to expand its traffic due to its inherent fuel efficiencies [but] success will be dependent upon the abilities to provide the service necessary to capture and retain such competitive movements," says Missouri Pacific President J. W. Gessner.

Adds Benjamin F. Biaggini, chairman of the Southern Pacific: "As fuel costs spiral, the railroads' inherent fuel economy will mean a significant bonus for the entire nation."

The railroad industry has just completed a second consecutive record year for traffic, with ton miles of about 900 billion compared with 858 billion in 1978, an increase of 4.9 percent.

In addition, the industry's financial condition improved, although it remains depressed in terms of profitability, when measured against other industry averages. The industry's rate of return on net investment for the twelve months ended September 30, 1979, was 2.53 percent compared with 0.94 percent the previous year and a 7 percent-to-11 percent level said to be adequate by federal regulators.

To be sure, industry-wide figures are distorted somewhat by inclusion of huge net losses attributed to several major railroads—Consolidated Rail Corp. (Conrail), a Northeast and Midwest giant that accounts for some 15 percent of all U.S. rail revenues, organized as a government-supported venture to replace bankrupt lines in the region; and two Midwest lines in bankruptcy, the Chicago, Milwaukee, St. Paul & Pacific (Milwaukee Road) and Chicago, Rock Island & Pacific (Rock Island) respectively the fifteenth- and sixteenth-largest railroads in 1978, in terms of revenues.

The Interstate Commerce Commission recently completed the second of its promised annual proceedings designed to determine adequate railroad revenue levels. There was good news and bad news—good in that the agency found necessary a return on net investment of 7 percent-to-11 percent, which should mean that the railroads in future years will be permitted to increase revenues to allow such a return on investment.

But the bad news was that only 13 of the 36 Class I railroads surveyed are earning adequate revenues and that 23 are not doing so. Since the railroad system needs to be restructured and slimmed down for yet more efficiency, the achievement of desired net investment return levels can't be accomplished rapidly, says the ICC.

"Rather, it is a goal toward which the carriers should be expected to move gradually as restructuring is accomplished, and as greater efficiency is attained through rate reforms and other measures," the ICC added. At the same time, it was noted that a 7 percent annual return is needed to provide sufficient flow of capital to make new investment profitable and to provide required equity capital from retained earnings. The industry itself calculates a fair return to be 12.6 percent.

Overall, there are 41 Class I linehaul railroads in the United States—railroads that have annual gross revenues of $50 million or more. These Class I railroads operate 92 percent of the total railway mileage in the country, employ 94 percent of the nation's railroad workers and handle 97 percent of the railway freight traffic (revenue ton-miles).

In addition to these major rail corporations, there are several hundred smaller companies that perform line-haul and/or switching and terminal services.

Two major nationwide rail systems serve Canada and connect at many points with various U.S.-based railroads. The railroads overall make up one big system, and some 70 percent of rail freight moves on more than one line.

In terms of commodities carried by the United States railroads last year, coal traffic was the heaviest in more than 25 years in terms of volume—surpassing the previous record in 1977 by 6.2 percent. Piggybacking—the movement of highway trailers on flatcars—set records in 1979 both for cars loaded and trailers/containers handled, for the third consecutive year, and piggyback revenues topped $1 billion for the first time.

Grain traffic also was the heaviest in history during the mid-June-to-December harvest season. The railroads moved an average of 95.3 million bushels a week compared with 85.9 million during the 1978 season, according to the Association of American Railroads.

These three areas—coal, grain, and piggyback shipping—are expected to be among the major sectors for booming business in the 1980s. John V. Pincavage, an analyst with the Wall Street investment firm of Paine Webber Mitchell Hutchins Inc., says many railroads will show above average real growth in business and regain some market share in this decade from increased carriage of coal and grain over long distances to utilities and to ports (for export) and from a higher share of general merchandise shipping via piggybacking. Box cars, a staple of railroads for a century of general merchandise shipping on their own, may well disappear in the new era of container shipping and increased cooperation with truckers for long-hauls.

To handle the increased business last year, locomotive and freight car fleets were expanded at rates not seen since the 1950s; freight car deliveries totaled about 85,000, the most since 1967; while locomotive deliveries exceeded 1,700, or the most since 1953, when the aging steam engine was being replaced by diesel power. With more new freight cars being added and fewer retired, there was a net gain of more than 40,000—the largest increase in 22 years and the first gain since 1976.

Booming business for new freight cars normally leads to a backlog of orders. After two years of heavy purchasing, suppliers have more than a year of orders in hand. The backlog of freight car orders is about 128,000—a ten-year high—with locomotive orders totaling about 800.

Among other industry developments:

—The railroads invested about $5 billion in capital improvements last year—about $3 billion for freight cars, more than $1 billion for engines and close to $1 billion for plant improvements.

—Safety records were improved—probably a direct result of the capital spending to improve rail roadbeds and installation of new ties and tracks. Train accidents in the first nine months of 1979 were down 11.2 percent from the same period of 1978, while derailments in the first three quarters fell by 13 percent to 5,757 from 6,617.

Says William H. Dempsey, the Association of American Railroads' president and chief executive officer: "The railroads made important advances on a number of different fronts in 1979 and the industry appears to be on the verge of a substantial long-term comeback when the national economy recovers."

On railroad profitability, Dempsey adds, "After four years on the brink of disaster, with earnings averaging no more than 1.4 percent on investment, we are at least moving in the right direction and I am hopeful that, in the long-term, this movement will continue."

Dempsey also agrees that the railroad industry in future years will reflect a consolidation now in progress through mergers. As a spokesman for all of the railroads, he is in the touchy position of not being able to speak for one or even a handful of the companies but he says, "You can see the dynamics going" in terms of current merger talk.

At the same time, Dempsey states that parceling out the Milwaukee Road and Rock Island systems is "a terrible way to purge the system." Still, some 96 percent of current Milwaukee traffic and 88 percent of current Rock Island traffic can be carried by competing railroads or state agencies that have made bids for various segments of the two failing lines.

"I don't feel we have any problems greater than we've had before," says Dempsey of an industry where there will be inevitable conflicts over some merger proposals and where there are opposing viewpoints about some elements of proposed industry deregulation. "The industry is remarkably united now after having been really divided before," he adds.

"Once the era of mergers is completed, an element of strain will be removed from the industry and everything we look at shows gains we can make together," Dempsey concludes.

ENERGY AND DEREGULATION

Railroad executives are concerned that in order for their industry to become really independent and profitable, the hand of government regulation must be reduced and public policy must recognize the energy-saving potential of railroad shipping.

An argument in favor of subsidizing the trucking industry (through government's assuming most of the burden of highway construction and repair) has been the rationale that trucking is more efficient. Now that is being questioned.

A recent Department of Transportation staff study found a ratio of about 3.8-to-1 in favor of railroads in terms of fuel efficiency in tons hauled. Battelle Institute (in a study for AAR) compared a direct rail route with a five-axle, heavy duty truck and found the railroad needed 500 British Thermal Units (BTUs) per net ton-mile while the truck needed 1,800. In net ton-miles per gallon that translates to 280 for the railroad and 77 for the truck.

However, the latest fuel efficiency study, released by the Department of Energy in January, concluded that there is "no single standard of comparison acceptable to all concerned and applicable on a general basis."

At the same time, DOE published data from a test of trucking versus railroads between Chicago and Minneapolis-St. Paul, based on new fast "sprint" trains.

Using twelve recorded intercity trips where simultaneous

information was available for truck and rail shipments, DOE
found:

	Truck	Rail
Distance (miles)	420	412
Speed (mph)	42.6	38.2
Fuel used (gallons)	82.3	1,283
Loaded/empty trailers	1/0	42/3
Gross ton-miles per gallon	117.7	257.8

Even if the recent DOE study was imperfect, it is apparent that for some portion of intercity freight the railroads
are more energy-efficient.

More research on modal fuel efficiency is required, but
trucks may be found less efficient for a significant portion of
their present business. This will force alterations in government policy that favors trucking.

Among the proposals made to correct public policy is an
intriguing idea from former Secretary of Transportation William T. Coleman Jr. He advocates a new Surface Transportation Trust Fund, to be financed by a 12 percent tax on fuel—
replacing the present 4 cent tax.

A percentage tax means that revenues would increase
with the price of fuel. And the income would be spent so:
one-third for highway construction, maintenance and safety;
one-third to metropolitan and rural areas to meet local needs;
and one-third for specific federal priorities, including the fos-
tering of cooperation for shipping by railroads and truckers
and for assistance to the railroads.

Such a plan, says Coleman, is needed for the U.S. "to
move into the next century with the kind of transportation
infrastructure and alternatives that we can truly afford." At
the same time, Coleman believes that deregulation of the rail
industry is less important.

"Reform that will not contribute significantly to a strong
national freight network would be like rearranging the deck
chairs on the Titanic," he says.

This year, in both the Senate and the House, real deregulation legislation has again been introduced, but the logjam of tough issues in an election year makes unlikely any final Congressional action.

With an Interstate Commerce Commission seated in Washington that is more attuned to the needs for easing regulation, the short-term outlook is that the railroads will end up with less regulation in the early 1980s—from the ICC itself and not from Congress.

WHERE ARE YOU, BENITO, NOW THAT WE NEED YOU?[2]

It was sunny as my train left Washington's Union Station last September. I was traveling to Boston to visit some old college friends, and I was in a good mood. My seat was comfortable, the interior of the car was modern, the woman sitting next to me was minding her own business. A few minutes out, I slipped off into a halfsleep, filled with memories of the places and friends I was returning to see. There was none of the wrenching and jostling, lurching and swaying I had grown accustomed to during my past few years as an Amtrak patron, and as reverie stole up on me the memories became more vivid. It was as if time had slowed its pace for my benefit . . . wait a minute. A glance at my watch confirmed my suspicions. Time was not standing still. All that had stopped was my train.

It had been close to an hour, I discovered, since my train—"The Minuteman"—had wrenched, jostled, lurched and swayed to a halt just south of Wilmington, Delaware. I was going to be late, but that came as no surprise. Delay has become a fact of life on the stretch of rail from Washington to Boston ever since Amtrak began the so-called Northeast Corridor Improvement Project (NECIP) four years ago. We pas-

[2] Reprint of article by Graham Beene. *Washington Monthly.* 12:51-8. Ap. '80. Reprinted with permission from The Washington Monthly. Copyright 1980 by the Washington Monthly Co., 2712 Ontario Road, N.W., Washington, D.C. 20009.

sengers are patient and tolerant, however, because we know the delays are all in a good cause—the best cause, you might say. For after a decade of trundling over a decaying roadbed at sub-automotive speeds, trying to meet fairy-tale timetables, Amtrak was finally bringing its trains into the Twentieth Century. That, at any rate, was what they told us on the cover of our schedules, which carried the prominent warning "Amtrak is undertaking major track rehabilitation on the Northeast Corridor. We regret any delays which may occur while this work progresses." That's what they repeated on the scripted announcements over the train loudspeaker, and that's what you heard when you dialed the handy phone number printed on the timetable to hear an apologetic recorded voice estimate the various delays along the route and thank you for your patience.

Most of all, that's what they had said back in 1976 when Congress passed the Railroad Revitalization and Regulatory Reform Act—commonly called the "4R Act." The Northeast Corridor project was part of that bill, and at the time, there hardly seemed to be anything that more clearly needed doing. The nation was coming out of Energy Crisis I, shocked at its vulnerability to a cut-off of oil supplies, determined, we told ourselves, not to let it happen again. Trains were the most fuel-efficient means of long-distance transportation around, everyone agreed. Of course the critics charged that people wouldn't ride them, that they loved their cars, that the trains restricted their mobility. No use pouring money down that hole, they said. Except for one place: the Northeast Corridor. There, even the critics agreed, the trains made sense. You had a string of cities close together—Boston, New Haven, New York, Philadelphia, Wilmington, Baltimore, Washington— not much question where most of the interstate travelers in that part of the country were going. And you had a population that was used to riding trains—had ridden trains, in fact, for decades, even in the face of declining service. Revitalize the service—smooth out the roadbed and get some of those really modern high-speed trains like they have in Japan running along this corridor—and it was a mortal lock you'd lure plenty of those urban Easterners out of their cars.

Thoughts like this were bubbling in Congress' brain when it passed, by a wide majority, a bill designating $3.6 billion for improvements along the Northeast Corridor. The legislation provided for an entirely new transportation system. Modern trains would pick up passengers at newly remodeled stations, whisking them to their destinations at speeds of 150 miles per hour. The trains would be quiet, smooth and reliable, and an entirely new track structure, with softened curves and a new electrification grid, would eliminate the maintenance headaches that have plagued Amtrak since its inception.

Unfortunately, a budget-conscious administration was not as smitten with this vision as Congress was, and President Ford openly stated he would veto the 4R Act if it ever reached his desk. The price was too high; [former] Transportation Secretary . . . Coleman called the proposed system a "luxury" the nation couldn't afford. By the time the Congress and the President struck a compromise, the cost of NECIP had been whittled down to a bargain-basement price of $1.75 billion. But the speed and the service this money would buy still sounded pretty mouth-watering to the average Amtrak passenger. In fact, in order to make sure the compromise 4R Act accomplished its purpose, Congress outlined in the statute itself what it had in mind. The project was to be completed quickly, by 1981. Once the curves were straightened and the roadbed improved, trains would be capable of reaching speeds of 120 miles per hour—fast enough!—and the trip times would be lowered to a reliable two hours and 40 minutes from Washington to New York, three hours and 40 minutes between New York and Boston. Since the trains regularly were taking four and five hours, respectively, to cover those same distances, it would be a pretty dramatic improvement—enough, the lawmakers anticipated, to attract 26.4 million energy-saving passengers a year instead of the 9.7 million riding in 1976. Finally, Congress wasn't about to give up on its 150-m.p.h. dreams; the act specified "the accomplishment of the required improvements in a manner compat-

ible with accomplishment in the future of additional improvements in service levels."

State officials along the corridor had other reasons for en-
dorsing the wonderful vision of the 4R Act. They called it the
most beneficial public works effort in their region. As the railroads opened up the West a century ago, the corridor project
would redeem the Northeast. With trip times slashed, it
would be faster to ride than to fly (counting time to and from
the terminals), relieving saturated airports and making them
safer and more efficient. Radically improved passenger and
freight capacity would stem the Northeast's outflow of population and industry—the railway, NECIP proponents said,
was a "spine" supporting the sagging infrastructure of the region. One New Jersey transportation official likes to recall the
wreathed funeral train of Robert Kennedy moving slowly
down the corridor, past the crumbling, dilapidated stations of
Trenton, Wilmington, and Baltimore. To him, that summed
up the plight of the whole area. NECIP was going to relieve
the sadness.

Well, forget it. Less than a year away from its alleged
completion date, NECIP is a shambles. Only a small fraction
of the proposed work has actually been completed. More important, it is becoming increasingly clear that many of the improvements envisioned by Congress will never be completed.
The congressional dreams of a fuel-efficient, modern rail system—the same dreams that console the Amtrak passengers
listening to explanations of the latest delay—will remain just
that.

All Aboard. . . .

When NECIP was signed into being by Gerald Ford in
1976, overall responsibility for the project was given to the
Federal Railroad Administration, a branch of the Department
of Transportation created in 1968 to develop a national policy on rail transportation. Now it is tempting to assume that
an agency named the Federal Railroad Administration will
have a lot of people on its staff who know about railroads. But

the truth is more subtle. The agency has only eight people within its staff of 75 who have any railroad background, and only four of those are in the 40-person NECIP project office. What kind of experience do the rest of the FRA officials have? They are very good at building highways. An agreement between the Federal Highway Administration and the FRA allows the two agencies to borrow staff from each other should one be caught shorthanded, as FRA was when the Northeast Corridor Project started. (So although this arrangement currently means that our railroads are being built by highway experts, it theoretically would allow us, at some point in the future, to enjoy highways planned by railroad experts.)

What about Amtrak, the National Railroad Passenger Corporation that actually operates trains on the corridor? Amtrak was to be the FRA's chief contractor, with responsibility for performing the vital track work. The two agencies were not an ideal match, however. In fact, over the years they had come to regard each other with a measure of suspicion, if not outright distrust. Amtrak tended to see FRA as a short-sighted group of budget-cutters who regarded trains as a "luxury." For FRA's part, it saw Amtrak as unaccountable, independent of federal control except when it was asking for public money to cover its soaring deficit. Amtrak had experience with railroads, all right—and those experiences were one of the reasons the FRA wanted to keep tight control over NECIP.

Moreover, whatever experience Amtrak had running railroads, it had little experience in *building* them, particularly not in a project of NECIP's magnitude, undertaken on a "live" track used by both freight and passenger trains. So FRA looked at Amtrak, and Amtrak looked at FRA warily, at arm's length and they both came to the conclusion that neither knew how to repair the Northeast Corridor. Then they did the only logical thing: they hired a contractor to do it for them. In this case the contractor was DeLeuw, Cather, Parsons Associates (DCP), a large architectural/engineering consortium. DCP would provide the project's overall design, as well as inspect Amtrak's construction work to make sure it was done right.

The arrangement did not get off to a propitious start. In fact, during the first full year of the five-year project *no* construction work was completed. It seems that after the 4R Act was passed, FRA had $1.75 billion and five years to spend it, but no plan for how to turn that money and time into a better rail system. "Planning" is one of those words that managerial types use so often that the rest of us begin to think it is meaningless—but in this case it isn't. Before you build a railroad, it helps to know how you are going to do it. Someone has to decide where the track is going to go. If there is a curve you have to decide whether or not to straighten it. When the track comes to a river you have to decide if the existing bridge will be strong enough to keep the train from falling into the river; if not, you must decide whether to build a new bridge or fix the old one. You must design the bridges and curves, and arrange for the right materials to be in the right place at the right time. Even though the Northeast Corridor had been the object of sporadic study for 15 years and intense study for two, these questions struck FRA like Socratic revelations, and a full work season was consumed amassing designs, materials, and staff. In March 1977 the new transportation secretary, Brock Adams, publicly expressed displeasure with FRA's progress and pledged to get the project underway if he had to do "pick and shovel work" on it himself. Still, it wasn't until August of that year that FRA produced the first listing of the specific bridges, curves, and sections of track that were to be improved.

And it was only when track work finally got started, in 1977, that everyone involved with the project began to realize it was in trouble. The problem, NECIP officials would later testify, was "unclear lines of authority," "a cross-confusion over roles and responsibilities." In simpler language, none of the three agencies knew what it was supposed to be doing, a result that might have been anticipated by anyone who looked at the convoluted relationship between the FRA, Amtrak, and DCP. Running the project would have been difficult enough even if each organization had a history of close cooperation with the others. But the truth was exactly the opposite, and the arrangement came to be known as the "three-headed monster." What FRA planned turned out to be different from what DCP designed, which in turn bore little resemblance to what Amtrak actually built. No one who worked on the project was particularly surprised, for example, when Amtrak installed 50,000 ties that failed to meet FRA specifications. (Rather than delay construction, Amtrak continued to accept and install the ties. The problem was finally resolved—by lowering the specifications.) And, although the DCP-FRA contract gave DCP "responsibility" for NECIP "implementation," even if the contractors saw Amtrak workers installing the ties upside down, they could not direct them to do the job right. DCP had no authority over Amtrak crews. Instead of preventing deficient work, DCP could only report it to FRA, which could then direct Amtrak to correct any construction inadequacies.

As the work proceeded from crisis to crisis, progress—despite the full year of planning—was abysmal. In 1977, the first year of actual construction, Amtrak completed only 54.5 percent of the track work planned for that year, at 130 percent of the budgeted cost. In 1978 progress improved somewhat—to 57 percent completed at 83 percent of budget. At that rate, the Union Pacific would have nailed the Golden Spike about the same day Greyhound opened its San Francisco bus terminal. But this wasn't like the old days, when all it seemed to take to build a railroad was several hundred indigent laborers, an engineer, and a foreman with a shotgun. Modern railroads are different, and between the DCP officials who negotiated with the FRA officials, who in turn directed the Amtrak officials, NECIP had established a new labor/management ratio. During the 1978 work season approximately 1,700 people were managing the project (800 in DCP alone) while only about 1,300 people were out on the tracks doing construction work.

Meanwhile, other problems were cropping up. A DCP review of Amtrak's purchases found almost $3 million in ties, rails, and other materials in excess of project requirements. Amtrak's own internal audit turned up inaccurate payroll records and erroneous production reports, including a $16-million discrepancy between the equipment and spare parts shown on the books and what was in the warehouses. The confusion was probably only the result of shoddy bookkeeping, but Amtrak, unable to untangle its own records, called in the FBI. A call to the FBI field office in Philadelphia will find the Bureau still untangling.

As these annoying little tales began to spread, the three principal actors began to snipe at each other. "I think they are up to their ears" (Amtrak president Paul Reistrup, referring to the FRA); ". . . has not demonstrated the ability to plan, supervise, and execute work with even a remote semblance of good management," (a DCP employee referring to Amtrak). But they did more than squabble—they took action. For one thing, they reorganized. FRA has had four NECIP directors since the 4R Act was passed, and Amtrak's Northeast Corridor division has undergone at least eight reorganizations since 1976. As a result, at any given moment a large percentage of NECIP employees are either new, inexperienced, or making arrangements to leave. "There is no such thing as job continuity on the Northeast Corridor," one Amtrak official stated.

For its part, FRA took the next logical step: it hired three contractors to oversee the work of the first contractor, DCP (whose job it was, remember, to oversee Amtrak). These additional contractors have cost $14.3 million, but the value of their contribution is in dispute. The consulting firm of Arthur Andersen, for example, was retained to develop "management systems" for NECIP. FRA and Amtrak were unable to agree on the value of Andersen's advice, however, and it was ignored—after $3 million had been spent. A GAO report, issued in early 1979, concluded tersely that "the contractors—except DCP—hired to provide technical expertise for FRA should be terminated."

The GAO report caught FRA by surprise, and the agency

decided to respond firmly. It summoned both DCP and Amtrak to the negotiating table to hammer out a "Memorandum of Understanding," allocating once and for all responsibility for the Northeast Corridor. A line from the "MOU," as it is called, captures its flavor: "As contractor to FRA, DCP acts as an extension of FRA, but has no authority to act for FRA in FRA relationships with Amtrak except through specific delegations of authority made by FRA to DCP with the consent of Amtrak." But Amtrak's responsibility couldn't be nailed down so simply. There is, for example, the following provision: "In recognition of the uncertainties associated with work on a live railroad, Amtrak's obligation to perform work within schedule and budget estimates is explicitly limited to the exercise of its best efforts." This isn't what lawyers would call an ironclad guarantee. An "amended MOU" is on the way.

Redirect Your Expectations

Such efforts came too late, however. The delays and waste during the first two years of the project assured that it couldn't be completed within the time, or the budget, specified in the 4R Act. So in 1979, the Department of Transportation completed a "Project Redirection Study" that confronted this reality, and the FRA translated the most important parts of the study into legislation now before Congress. Among other things, the "Northeast Corridor Completion Act of 1979" redirects the completion date of the project five years into the future (although the clock doesn't start ticking until the legislation is passed, so even if Congress acted tomorrow, NECIP wouldn't be finished until 1985). It also redirects an additional $750 million into the project, although there seems to be little pretense within the project's management that this will see it through to completion. As the FRA cheerfully explained: "The estimates generated under the redirection effort reflect the best and most accurate now available; however, no illusion of precision should be inferred. Projects of this size always have surprises, usually unpleasant." Or, as a DCP engineer told me, "$750 million is just not going to be enough."

Of course, cost overruns—particularly with inflation climbing through the teens—are about as surprising these days as a courtroom confession in the closing minutes of *Perry Mason*. And, in fairness to the guilty, the 4R Act's original budget figure of $1.75 billion was probably selected more because it was agreeable to both Congress and the Ford administration than because it bore a relationship to any specific package of improvements to be carried out on the Corridor. The route was originally constructed in the nineteenth century, and has been neglected for decades by the failing railroads that operated along the corridor before the federal government stepped in in the early '70s. The cost of performing the deferred maintenance alone has probably exceeded a billion dollars.

The average Amtrak rider, twiddling his thumbs on a siding in Wilmington, and the average driver guzzling his way along the New Jersey turnpike because he didn't have time to wait on that siding, probably would have the same reaction to the cost overruns: Who cares? As long as the damn thing gets built, and I can get to New York in less than three hours, what's a little overrun? (The Japanese, after all, are spending as much for a single tunnel in their high-speed system as we're spending on the entire Northeast Corridor.) In fact, since the inflation that has helped drive up NECIP's costs is caused, in large part, by the skyrocketing price of the very oil an efficient train system would save, you could argue the system has become *more* necessary, even as its costs have risen.

That's why the heart of the NECIP fiasco is not just how much money it's costing, but what we're getting for our money—which, in short, is nothing like what we were told we were getting. At each stage, as the "three-headed monster" that runs NECIP consumed more time and money, the FRA reacted by paring down the "scope" of the project. I don't mean paring down the $3.6-billion "luxury" budget killed by the Ford administration, but from the $1.75-billion project finally authorized. This was the third element of the "project redirection," the quiet lowering of expectations. The process in itself has meant wasted money, since FRA has eliminated proposed improvements that it had already paid DCP to design (a GAO sampling found that 40 percent of NECIP's design dollars went for projects that will not be completed).

But mainly it means that we should forget the vision of dramatically improved, high-speed rail service along the Northeast Corridor. In a different atmosphere, the FRA might have been able to go to Congress and say, "Look, this project is more necessary than ever, and this is what we will need to finish it." But by now a promise from the Iranian government to finish the job would have as much credibility on Capitol Hill; NECIP has the smell of a boondoggle about it, offering little assurance that money spent on the project will be translated into better rail service rather than more embarrassment. The original budget has been frittered away, and Congress isn't about to authorize any more than it can get away with.

So forget, for example, the idea of soaring new bridges that avoid the need for Amtrak's trains to slow down as they speed to their destinations. When first planned in 1977, the project was to replace or rehabilitate over 400 bridges along the corridor. But when its money began to disappear, FRA axed $188 million from the budget—and 151 bridges in need of repairs were allowed to stay the way they were. Of the bridges that will still get NECIP's attention, half of the ones that were to be replaced are only going to be repaired.

Of the bridges cut from the project, some desperately need fixing. One of these crosses the Hackensack River in the New Jersey Meadowlands. Pieces of its superstructure are missing, and what remains is seriously rusted. Bolts are loose or gone entirely, and the main pier is severely damaged, having been rammed by an occasional barge. A DCP engineer with whom I spoke apologized for not being able to provide more details, but his own visit to the bridge had been cut short when a rotted tie almost dropped him into the river.

At hearings before the House Government Activities and Transportation subcommittee, James A. Caywood, DCP's Northeast Corridor Project director, put the bridge problem in more abstract, but barely reassuring, terms: "We have it down to a pretty low level; it will be all right, it will be safe, as long as Amtrak has the money to maintain their property. If they don't, and we don't fix these bridges up under the improvement program, we are going to have troubles.

Then there are those curves that were supposed to be straightened. The effect of curves on the operation of a railroad is more subtle than that of dilapidated bridges. While curves don't have the potential for interrupting your commute with an early morning dip in the Hackensack, they do have a major impact on the speed and reliability of the system as a whole. If a curve is too sharp, a train can't go around it very fast without, as Mr. Caywood would say, having troubles. That's one big reason why Amtrak's Metroliners, which have a top speed capability of around 115 m.p.h. in a straight line, average only around 64 m.p.h. Other curves will allow trains to run at high rates of speed, but only by taking a high toll on the passengers' insides. Finally, the higher the speed and the sharper the curve, the greater the forces applied to the track and the more maintenance it needs.

For these reasons, the August 1977 plan included 212 curves that were to be "realigned"—either straightened, allowing higher speeds, or banked to reduce the rollercoaster effect on the passengers. That number has now been cut to 41, all of them mere bankings. The plans to actually short-cut severe bends were scotched because they would have required the track to leave Amtrak's right-of-way, necessitating expensive purchases of land. The "realignments" that are left will not save time; they will only smooth out some of the curves with high stomach-turning potential (high "jerk rates"). But the other curves, along with several that will now be banked instead of straightened, will still provide ample opportunities for nausea. And some major Amtrak bottlenecks—like the bend on the approach to the Bay View Bridge near Baltimore, where trains must slow to 30 miles per hour—will hardly be touched at all. (The biggest bottleneck on the whole corridor, the Baltimore Tunnel—built in 1873 and too narrow to handle a freight and a passenger train at the same time—was never even scheduled by FRA for replacement. The speed limit in the tunnel was recently lowered to 10 m.p.h. Under NECIP, its drainage and lighting will be improved.)

Of course, all the future maintenance that will be needed to patch up the bridges that aren't being replaced, and the curves that must bear higher loads, means that even the economy of the project's truncation may be questioned—to say nothing of the future passengers who will sit in idle trains while Amtrak crews do repair work. FRA has taken this factor into account, however—and *reduced* the number of maintenance bases along the corridor by 60 percent, against the advice of Amtrak's Japanese high-speed rail experts.

But what about the commuter's bottom line, namely how long it will take to get there? Congress knew what would attract riders to the trains, which is why they went so far as to write the projected trip times into the 4R Act itself. The goals they came up with weren't all that tough—2 hours and 40 minutes from Washington to New York averages out to around 85 m.p.h. including stops. For comparison, as recently as 1969 the Penn Central offered a nonstop train that beat this time by ten minutes.

But with all the curves that are staying curved, and the bridges left on the drawing boards, it's difficult to see how even these schedules will be met. In fact, they probably won't be, at least not on any steady basis. You won't catch the FRA admitting this—precisely because the trip times are written into law, the FRA has treated them as holy writ, even to the extent of justifying the project's "redirection" on the grounds that Amtrak will still be able to meet the statutory timetable.

"Trip times," however, are a more flexible concept than they might at first seem. A railroad can make any given train meet a tight schedule through a number of tricks—cutting out station stops (as in 1969), shunting all the other freight and passenger traffic onto sidetracks until the priority train rolls through. On the Northeast Corridor, this sort of scheduling can cut an hour from a Washington-N.Y. trip. But there's a big difference between having a few special trains meeting a tight schedule—in the process delaying all the other trains by making them step aside—and building a system where all trains can consistently meet that same timetable. It's a difference Amtrak is counting on. Even so, they're not signing anything in blood. As Reistrup testified: "I would hope, personally . . . that we should have at least a minimum number of schedules in the timetable, particularly in the business hours, let's say morning, noon, and evening, that would meet the 2 hour and 40 minute, 3 hour and 40 minute goals."

Given the fudge factor built into "trip times," the best gauge of how fast Amtrak's service will be is probably its "reliability standards," the measure of how many trains will actually meet the advertised schedules. So you should know that the reliability standards for the improved Northeast Corridor service have been steadily reduced, from "95-percent-within-five-minutes" when NECIP started, to the current hope that 85 percent of the trains will be no more than ten minutes late. But those are abstract statistics. To get a handle on them, it helps to know that the "85-10" reliability standard that will be used on the finished corridor is the same as the standard Amtrak uses now. Ask any rider what great service that is.

Finally, there is what happens beyond 1985. Congress was concerned about that future—remember those visions of 150-m.p.h. trains and the provisions in the 4R Act calling for "the accomplishment of . . . improvements in a manner compatible with accomplishments in the future of additional service levels"? The lawmakers may have been thinking of Japan's national railroad, which has been running trains at over 135 m.p.h. since the mid-sixties. Or the French—when their new Paris-Lyons line goes into service next year it will operate at speeds of 160 m.p.h. In 1978, a congressional committee asked DCP's Caywood about this statutory goal of future improvements. His response: "My interpretation of that is that there was an initial objective of hoping that we could design toward 150-miles-an-hour speed. These things have long gone by the board. . . . No major expansion of system capacity is planned at any point on the Corridor."

A Strange Electricity

But if the system can't expand its capacity for speed, surely it will expand its capacity for people. That, after all, is the point of the whole exercise: attracting an expected 26.4 million riders by 1990. But a chain, they say, is only as strong as its weakest link—and the weak link of the Northeast Corridor, as far as people-carrying capacity is concerned, is the antique electrification system running along the southern leg from New York to D.C. It uses electricity of a peculiar voltage that is produced by the railroad's own power plants. Electricity of this type isn't generated commercially anywhere else on earth. The system is extremely prone to failure—and it cannot handle the dramatic increase in passengers the NECIP project is designed to stimulate.

To cure this defect, the FRA had planned a new electrification system that could handle more power, higher speeds, and would be more reliable because it would draw current from nearby commercial grids. Guess what is not being built. Without the new system, those 26.4 million people won't be able to ride the trains in 1990 even if they want to. No doubt there will be appropriate, preprinted messages handed to them as they shuffle back to their cars and drive off onto the highway, burning up their precious $8-a-gallon gasohol: "Amtrak is undertaking major track rehabilitation on the Northeast Corridor . . . we regret any inconvenience. . . ."

DEREGULATION OF THE RAILROADS[3]

Passage of the Staggers Rail Act last October [1980] was supposed to move the nation's rail carriers down much the same "deregulation" road the airlines have taken. At the moment, however, it's doubtful that the 1,800 bureaucrats that

---

[3] Excerpt from article entitled "This Place Is a Complete Zoo," by Barbara Rudolph, reporter-researcher. *Forbes.* 12:122–3. Ap. 27, '81. By permission of Forbes Magazine Inc., © 1981.

make up the Interstate Commerce Commission are hard at work behind their Doric columns on Constitution Avenue in Washington making themselves unnecessary. For three months the ICC, the nation's oldest and most hidebound regulatory agency, has been without a chairman. At the moment, 6 of the 11 seats on the commission are vacant. ICC staffers, of course, will play critical roles in determining what the new legislation really means. But today, six months after it was passed, no one yet has much of an idea.

Some things can be easily inferred, of course. The rails, for example, are not likely to see the same chaos that swept the airline industry after its deregulation: Airlines can easily enter and escape a particular market, but railroads cannot pick up their tracks and move into a new territory.

Even so, many railroaders still fear price wars will break out in the months ahead. Warns Union Pacific President William Cook, "There could be a bloodbath for a while if someone cuts the hell out of rates to buy business." Should a bloodbath occur, the better-capitalized companies—especially rich western lines like BN, Sante Fe and UP—are likely to get stronger while their weaker brethren fall by the wayside or become candidates for acquisition.

Since passage of the Reed-Bullwinkle Act of 1948, railroads had enjoyed a special competitive advantage: They had been permitted to meet with one another and set rates without fear of antitrust prosecution. Through four major regional rate bureaus, carriers established tariffs. Once these were approved by the ICC they seemed cast in bronze—no surprise rate cuts to boost market share.

Now, under the 1980 Staggers Rail Act, railroaders are beginning to set rates independently, and—starting next January—they will lose their antitrust immunity. That prospect sends chills up the spines of not a few industry executives. As one railroader put it, "This is a tremendous change for us. We must now get a real handle on costs, which is something many of us have never done before."

Indeed, equating of costs with rates has rarely been a strong point under ICC regulation. Back in the mid-1970s, for example, the ICC approved a general 7 percent increase in freight rates. At first glance it seemed certain to bolster railroad profit margins. But, unfortunately, the fine print contained exemptions for 14 key commodities like cars and car parts, coal and fresh fruits. The rationale: The shippers of those commodities were in depressed industries and deserved a break. "It was as if the railroads were in such good shape they could afford to pick up the burden for General Motors," says Constance Abrams, ICC associate director of policy and analysis, who vainly opposed the ruling. "It was a regulatory nightmare."

In other ways, too, the effect of deregulation is hard to forecast. For example, the ICC will now get involved in rate-setting only if proposed rates exceed costs by a certain percentage, and can even pull out altogether if it believes there's sufficient competition to protect shippers. Nowhere in the Staggers Act, however, is any definition of sufficient competition spelled out. That's just one area where the ICC's staff will have considerable influence.

RAILROADS:
OUT OF THE PAST AND INTO THE FUTURE[4]

America's highly touted interstate highway system is badly in need of repair, and deteriorating at an alarming rate. But rather than sink billions of dollars more into fixing an outmoded highway system made obsolete by energy costs even before its completion, the United States should seriously consider building an interstate *railroad* system of energy-efficient, high-speed, long-distance passenger trains. Japan has been operating them for years, carrying intercity travelers at 130 miles per hour. Similar service is now available in France, at 160 mph. By contrast, Amtrak's trains can't *begin* to attain

[4] Article by J. H. Foegen, professor of business, Winona State University. *Futurist.* 15:59–63. D. '81. By permission of the publisher, World Future Society, 4916 St. Elmo Avenue, Washington, D.C. 20014.

such speeds on present roadbeds—and its very existence has been threatened by budget cutbacks.

Granted, mass transit works better in relatively small, densely populated nations. And France and Japan are more dependent on imported oil than the U.S. is—a situation that naturally encourages efficient fuel use. Nevertheless, escalating oil prices are reason enough to reconsider long-distance rail travel in the U.S. also. But even if OPEC guaranteed price stability for the next few decades, the cost of repairing or replacing present highways would be an excellent reason in itself.

The current alternatives to rail travel are becoming less satisfactory. Although air travel has become the dominant form of intercity travel by public carrier in the U.S., up from 3 percent of passenger miles in 1940 to 80 percent in 1979, given current and likely future conditions, such growth can hardly continue. Large jets use huge amounts of expensive fuel just to get airborne, not to mention reaching their destinations. Recognizing such diseconomies, a British parliamentary committee in 1981 recommended ending support for the supersonic Concorde, whose 1980 fuel costs accounted for 35 percent of total operating expenses.

Cars are still the most popular form of travel, accounting for about 85 percent of *all* (by public and private carrier) intercity passenger miles. While cars use less fuel as they become smaller, for the same reason they become much less comfortable for long trips. There *must* be a better way.

There is, or at least there could be—a thoroughly revamped railroad system, one that could do for twenty-first century travelers what a predecessor did earlier. Years ago, of course, railroads were the major carriers of cross-country passenger traffic. As recently as 1940, 60 percent of all such travel was by rail. Chicago's Pullman Company, now part of Wheelabrator-Frye, became famous by meeting the need for overnight accommodations. Later, diesel-powered streamliners replaced less efficient, coal-burning "steam-liners." (Might coal make a comeback here, too?) Eventually, however, the car's convenience and the plane's speed did such passenger trains in.

Today, it is painfully obvious that the cheap gasoline that made possible the popularity of car and plane travel is no longer available. The time has come, therefore, to build a new, high-speed rail network that would essentially replace the present interstate highways. "Superhighways" have had their day; because of the overriding fuel consideration, "super rail" has to be tomorrow's mode.

Obsolete Before Completion

Until now, the 40,000-mile interstate highway system (or "I-system") has been the pride of an extensive road network. A mere 1 percent of the country's 4 million miles of roads, it handles almost 20 percent of all traffic. After decades of construction, 94 percent of it is now open.

Unfortunately, with heavy use and inadequate maintenance, the system is going downhill rapidly. According to a 1981 General Accounting Office report, "It's percentage of miles in poor condition more than doubled over the last three reporting years. Billons of dollars will be needed to preserve these roads, and if timely action is not taken, deterioration will accelerate and even more money will be needed for reconstruction." Almost three-fourths of the network is already obsolete by modern road standards, and the Federal Highway Administration estimates that, overall, it is wearing out at an annual rate 50 percent faster than it is being replaced. In 1975, about 73 percent of its mileage was in good condition. By 1978, this figure had fallen to 62 percent, while 29 percent was in fair condition and 9 percent in poor (needing resurfacing or reconstruction). Even in fair condition, roads fall apart fast.

Inflation adds to the problem. Construction costs have risen 145 percent since 1970, maintenance 105 percent. In fact, the General Accounting Office report noted that, as of January 1980, the cost of completing the remaining

2,500 miles of the I-system would be an estimated $53.8 billion, nearly double the initial estimate for the whole 40,000 miles!

Highway Revenues Can't Keep Pace

Revenues from highway-user taxes have not kept pace, rising only 60 percent since 1970, roughly half the combined rate of building and maintenance costs. Twenty years ago, the average state gasoline tax of 5.9 cents was 19 percent of the price of gasoline, but by 1980 the tax of about 8.3 cents was only 7 percent of the gas price.

Compounding the dilemma, the I-system is only *part* of a much larger road network also needing upkeep. Governments at all levels spent over $600 billion on roads during the past 60 years, with an aggregate replacement cost for this network estimated at up to $3 trillion. States will require an estimated $67 billion over the next 20 years to maintain their non-interstate highways. All this money must ultimately come from the same source, taxpayers.

Admittedly, it will also cost billions to build the proposed high-speed rail system. If people want to move, there is no longer a cheap way. The only real question is, On *what* is it wiser to spend the extra billions that will inevitably be required—on a badly deteriorating highway system built for cheap gasoline and gas-guzzling V-8's, or on new or upgraded rail more in tune with today's fuel realities?

The situation's logic demands greater use of rail. Good though it once was, the I-system has become energy obsolete as well as increasingly decrepit physically. By nature, it encourages greater gasoline use by making possible higher speeds. Some Western states, in fact, have argued vigorously for repeal of the 55-mile-an-hour limit as inappropriate for their wide open spaces. One legislature passed a measure imposing a whopping $5 fine on speeders; the letter of federal law is honored, but hardly the spirit.

If good roads are available, people will want more cars and will use the ones they have more intensively than if roads are poor—a fact so obvious that it is often overlooked. More cars, traveling more miles, at faster speeds, all encouraged by good highways, make for a continuing high rate of gas consumption ever more difficult to afford.

Railroad Savings

Even today, railroads, devoted mostly to hauling large-volume, high-density freight, are for many reasons a lower-cost, less-energy-using means of transport. The friction of steel wheels on steel rails is less than that of rubber on concrete. A railroad car weighing 20 tons, in fact, can almost be moved on track by one person pushing on it. A train faces air resistance only once for its entire length, not once for each unit as with motor vehicles. Unlike cars and planes, trains run efficiently on electricity that can be generated using a variety of fuels. According to a National Science Foundation study published in 1973, supported by another by the U.S. Department of Transportation in 1979, trains are about one-fourth as energy intensive as trucks. Trains have a greater capacity, as well. A railroad track can accommodate double-decker trains carrying 2,000 people every two minutes—at least 10 times more than what would be possible if all those people rode in cars.

Energy savings would at *some* speed be subject to diminishing returns. According to German government research, rail technology has an advantage up to 185 miles an hour. If pushed much beyond that, the cost of maintenance and energy becomes prohibitive. In upgrading present rail in this country, however, such limits are unlikely to be a practical concern for years.

Contrary to popular belief, people *are* still willing to ride trains. For example, the fabled Orient Express, restored to its original splendor, began running again in September 1981 from Istanbul to Milan. And in South Africa, the "Blue Train," said to be the world's most luxurious, required reservations months in advance to enjoy its lavishly carpeted compartments, showers, valet service, and excellent food.

On a more mundane level, Amtrak still operates a 22,000-mile network of passenger service, although it has serious financial problems. The Reagan administration, for instance, contending that most of its trains aren't economically justified, at one point proposed cutting the budget so deeply as to leave only the Boston-Washington corridor intact. Amtrak President Alan S. Boyd sprang quickly to the defense, arguing that "in the midst of a heated debate over whether or not this country needs a nationwide rail passenger system, it is important for the public to understand that Amtrak is experiencing unprecedented demand for rail passenger service." He cited sold-out accommodations, reservation center waiting lists, and over 40 percent of coach seats on reserved trains nationwide being booked two weeks in advance. Subsequently, reportedly due to homefront political pressure and a strong desire to get the 1982 budget passed in complete form, the administration made more money available. Boyd then said that the $735 million voted, though down considerably from the $900 million of the year before, would permit continued operation of 85 percent of the system.

Trains Racing Around the World

In addition to the fuel efficiency of rail, and the actual and potential number of riders, there is ample precedent for developing high-speed passenger trains. Other countries have been developing them aggressively, even to the extent of threatening some markets formerly dominated by planes. Journey time, rather than just speed, is the key. On intermediate-length routes, trains can have an edge if state-of-the-art technology is used, since rail terminals can be located close to population centers while remotely located airports require substantial access time through congested urban traffic, often canceling much of the plane's speed advantage.

First to develop such high-speed trains were the Japanese, whose 130-mile-an-hour Shinkansen line has operated since 1964. A second generation is being built, with anticipated speeds up to 160.

In England, British Rail currently runs a diesel High

Speed Train carrying normal intercity traffic at up to 125 mph. It is developing an electrified Advanced Passenger Train, designed to reach 155, to be introduced by 1984 on its London-Glasgow route.

France holds the world rail speed record of 236 mph, set on February 26, 1981. Its new TGV Train ("Tres Grande Vitesse," or "very great speed") has cut the time between Paris and Lyon to a mere 2 hours, already causing one domestic airline serving the route to plan cutbacks. There are only two stops in the 265 miles, since it takes 3 miles to break at 160 mph, and a 3-minute stop loses 18 minutes in schedule time.

Germany also has trains running at up to 125 mph, and is developing magnetic levitation technology to more than double that. The Ministry of Research and Technology is developing a system capable of going 300 mph, as well as an experimental 220 mph train designed to push to the limits of the steel-wheel-on-steel-rail technology.

Potentially dangerous problems arise when rail speeds get into these ranges. In Germany one winter, 125 mph service was cut to "only" 100 after ice flew up from beneath one high-speed train and broke 40 windows in another that was passing. At speeds of around 185, conventional wheel flanges are not enough to keep trains safely on track. One way to keep these high-speed trains under control is to build a high, concrete center curb that the train straddles much as a rider does a horse.

Regardless of the problems, the potential of high-speed rail is apparent. The challenge is there, pushed by the high cost of fuel, if not pulled by national pride.

So far, U.S. involvement has been slow. A few states, such as California and Ohio, have been active. And a research arm of the Federal Railroad Administration has been monitoring overseas developments, sending officials abroad since 1973, in case the country should one day want to go this route. Congress authorized planning funds in 1978, but the Reagan administration has not been enthusiastic. The Department of Transportation still sees even the most likely corridor, from Boston to Washington, as serving commuters, not business or other travelers.

Interestingly enough, Amtrak has been trying to interest private investors, here and abroad, in building routes to accommodate Japanese-type fast trains. A private Japanese investor recently agreed to finance a $5 million feasibility study of four "bullet" train routes: Los Angeles–San Diego, Chicago–Detroit, Houston–Dallas, and Tampa–Orlando–Miami. Though the cost of building them would be in the billions, Amtrak's president thinks that in some markets the company could cover operating costs and repay construction loans. Sporadically threatened by budget cutbacks, Amtrak could yet turn near-defeat into victory if somehow it could sell and implement this idea.

Highway Soil Bank

If a high-level decision were made favoring high-speed rail over continued maximum support of the interstate highway system, a related one would be needed about what to do with the present highway system. One possibility would be to maintain half the system while allowing the other half to "lie fallow." Two lanes would be kept in service, functional but with no frills. The other two would not be maintained. Rather, they would be seen as a temporarily paved over, strategic reserve of potential farmland, a new kind of soil bank.

A step in this direction is already being taken. Farmers with winning bids made to the Minnesota Department of Transportation harvest hay along selected stretches of interstate right-of-way. A Massachusetts dairy operator mows hay between runways of a Boston airport.

Such a reserve of farmland could one day be vital, since world food problems are expected to become even more critical than they are today. U.S. farmers will have to plant between 84 and 143 million more acres by the year 2000 to meet anticipated foreign and domestic food demand, according to government estimates. But the Agriculture Department reports that 3 million acres a year—an area roughly the size of Connecticut—is converted from actual or potential cropland to nonfarm use. Already, the World Bank says 800 million people in developing nations are not able to feed themselves, even minimally. And the Presidential Commission on World Hunger has concluded that a food crisis more serious than that involving energy could develop over the next few decades. Among other recommendations, it urges setting up international grain reserves, a U.S. emergency wheat reserve, and improved U.S. government policies to strengthen the agricultural system.

Although there was much criticism of "paving over good farmland" when interstate highways were being built, it might have unknowingly been fortunate in the long run. Reserving those thousands of acres in fallow condition beneath concrete all these years leaves an "ace in the hole" for when food needs become more critical. (In a sense, land has been saved in a "mile a month" plan, as many save money through the bond a month program.)

In a related comparison, many cities used to rely on "trolley cars" for mass transit. (Today, they are called "light rail," and may be coming back. Pittsburgh is completing a new system costing nearly half a billion dollars. Philadelphia ordered 141 new lightweight cars from Japan. And San Diego bought 14 cars and is laying 25 kilometers of track.) Eventually, the flexibility and popularity of buses made them all but disappear. Their tracks were often paved over as the least expensive way to get rid of them. During World War II, tracks were dug up for vitally needed scrap metal. Some day in the future, people might be just as glad to be able to dig up badly needed farmland, buried for years beneath highways.

History does repeat itself, often with a touch of irony. Railroads, which once enjoyed a near-monopoly on long-distance passenger travel over land, flowered in such glamorous and comfortable streamliners as the Twentieth Century Limited and the Hiawathas. Later, they were edged out by car and plane, seemingly relegated to a quaint niche, a fading image of old-fashioned, lumbering stodginess. They could, however, still pass their rivals, capitalizing not only on fuel economy in a conserving age, but on new technology capable of competitive speeds.

THE MASS TRANSIT ALTERNATIVE

EDITOR'S INTRODUCTION

"Traffic congestion, traffic accidents, air pollution, parking problems, overtaxed facilities for vehicle service and repair, and the disruption of cities by highway construction projects." More than a decade ago, a speaker cited these well-known automobile problems to his audience. While his listeners may have nodded knowingly to these familiar complaints, their eyebrows must have initially furrowed at the candor of the speaker, Henry Ford II.

More than ever, there is a tendency today to apply the 1960s catchphrase, the American automobile is no longer part of the solution but part of the problem. This section surveys the growing number of urban transportation alternatives to the car.

In the first article, Professor James Wheeler of the University of Georgia examines, from a geographical standpoint, the history of the American commuter and his dependence on the automobile. He points out that the public transport decline in the twentieth century, due to the spread of people and activities throughout the metropolitan space, was encouraged by federal policy. In the next selection, a speech by Daphne Christensen entitled "Autos and Mass Transit," she concurs with this view in comparing the effects of urban transit legislation with federal highway legislation and she discusses the need for more transportation planning. Examples of such planning can be found in the next article, "How Cities Are Coaxing People Out of Their Cars," reprinted from *U. S. News & World Report.* It describes seven transportation programs designed to discourage the use of cars in a variety of municipalities, including Seattle, Minneapolis-St. Paul, and Syracuse. In the fourth article from the *Journal of the Institute for Socioeconomic Studies,* William J. Ronan, former chairman of the MTA, discusses the "Transit Renaissance" and analyzes the reasons for the "fiasco" in the manufacture of buses and trains.

Then, in considering another alternative to the car, "Rumbling Toward Ruin," reprinted from *Time*, surveys the dismal economic plight of the nation's decaying mass transit systems, while "Sick and Inglorious Transit," also from *Time*, looks at the increasing fares that the harried commuter must pay. Finally, the idea of a no-fare transit, first proposed in Boston in 1922, has enjoyed renewed attention by Joe Brady, who regards transit as an "essential public service." He reports in the *AFL-CIO American Federationist* on the effects of no-fare experiments on ridership.

THE LONG, LONG TRAIL TO WORK[1]

Much of the social and economic fabric of life in the United States is woven around the daily commuter trip. Although this may apply to other nations as well, it applies uniquely to the USA, where the nature of commuter transport is quite different from the journey to work in other industrialized countries. The two principal characteristics setting the USA apart are the length and duration of commuter trips and the mode of travel. The impact of these characteristics, as they have operated for several decades, is a rather distinctive metropolitan landscape that is best described as de-concentrated.

In the early part of this century, when the cost and effort of moving people over distance was great, commuter trips were generally very short. The emerging urban landscape was rather compact. Accessibility was a prime commodity, and a central location for manufacturing, retailing and wholesaling was of paramount importance. The most accessible land was also the most valuable and attracted a host of centrally lo-

[1] Article by James O. Wheeler, head, department of geography, University of Georgia. *Geographical Magazine.* 53:511–16. My. '81. By permission of the publisher.

cated economic activities. This clustering of activities became known as the Central Business District, or C.B.D. Commuter trips, including many walking trips, were almost entirely focussed directionally upon the C.B.D., and their length tended to be relatively short. From 1890 to 1920, almost all US cities, even those having populations as low as 10,000 people, had electrically powered mass transit, known as the streetcar or the 'trolley'. Trolley routes, run over the street networks in most cases, dominated urban commuter transport.

During the 1920s the private automobile became popular and widespread in the USA. In the early years of automotive transport, the vehicle was unreliable, subject to numerous breakdowns, while the quality of both highways and city streets was very poor. With improvements in vehicles and road surfaces, the private automobile became a more common means of commuting, changing from a luxury to a necessity within a short span of years. The growth of the automobile was a principal, though not the only, reason for the slow but steady decline of electric traction street railways in US cities. Characteristically the street railways were in weak financial condition. More than anything else, government policy and public attitudes favoured highway financing and private automobile purchases.

The predominance of automobiles for commuting, despite increased congestion, pollution, and cost, has continued. Public transport underwent a profound decline, especially after World War II. Even though the advantages of the motorbus were greater than the electric streetcar, the bus came to be only a kind of auxiliary mode of travelling to work. During the first two decades of this century the number of commuters grew more rapidly than the urban population. The absolute number of passengers stabilized during the 1920s but automotive transport captured a growing share of the increasing urban transport market. During World War II commuting grew to the highest levels ever, because of the shortage of automobile parts and the rationing of petrol. However, as soon as the war was over and automobiles and parts became available once again, the number of passengers began a long-term plunge. Total ridership by 1970 was less than had existed in 1910, despite the major increases in urban population in those sixty years. Commuter transport became dependent upon 'peak-hour' commuters, as well as those who had access to no other form of transport. After World War II, the main type of commuter transport changed from the streetcar to the passenger bus, which currently accounts for approximately three-quarters of all commuter trips.

The post-war decline in commuting has been more noticeable in smaller cities than in larger metropolitan areas. Rapid transit systems, usually at least in part built in underground 'subways', are found in only a relatively few American metropolitan areas. The first rapid transit subway was constructed in Boston just before the turn of the century. New York City opened its subway in 1904, followed by Philadelphia, Chicago and Cleveland. The San Francisco Bay Area Rapid Transit, BART, was the first new rapid transit rail system to open in half a century. More recently, metropolitan areas such as Seattle, Washington, D.C., and Atlanta have opened rail rapid transit systems. Since the mid-1970s there has been a very modest increase in the number of passengers using mass transit, despite the emphasis on federally funded public transport programmes.

The result of the predominance of the automobile in US commuting, and the long average distances travelled, has been most noticeably felt on the geographical arrangement of metropolitan areas. From the compact urban area at the turn of the century in which work trips focussed almost entirely on the C.B.D., US metropolitan areas of the 1980s are an unwieldy, almost never ending scatter of activities and people over a broad region, including so-called non-metropolitan areas. If one plots the number of commuter trips of a given distance on one axis against distance on the other axis, a 'distance decay' effect will be observed. Thus, there will be a large number of trips going a short distance and a gradually decreasing number of trips going even longer distances. Such relationships led transport geographers and planners to observe that there is a tendency for one to minimize either travel time or distance. Others saw this minimization principle as a subset of a more general principle of 'least-effort' behaviours. The operation of such a principle of human behaviour has direct and obvious implications for the geographical arrangements of residence and facilities in metropolitan areas.

Careful curve-fitting of commuter data for US metropolitan areas over the past several decades has pointed up some interesting and surprising relationships. Data for the early-1950s, and by implication before then, show a steep distance decay line, indicating a rapid decrease in the number of work trips with increasing distance. Most people worked close to their homes. Several models were developed to demonstrate how the residential location decision was based on workplace location. The workplace, the majority of which were in the C.B.D., was viewed as the principal organizing factor in the geographical structure of the metropolitan area.

As work trip data became available during the 1960s and 1970s, a different picture began to emerge. The old principle of distance decay in general held but it did not accurately describe commuter trips of a relatively short distance. It was postulated that there existed a small 'frictionless' zone surrounding each household, within which distance was not considered to be a factor affecting travel behaviour. A trip of six kilometres was perceived to require as much travel effort as one of three kilometres. Such a finding had obvious implications for theories of urban spatial structure, since it implied that a household had a greater geographical choice of where to locate both the residence and the workplace. One other implication was that a rather small urban area might fall entirely within a frictionless zone, providing no travel constraints associated with choice of residence or workplace. The residential location decision could be based on other factors, such as amenities. Likewise, workplaces were free to relocate into suburban areas and certainly new workplace locations, whether manufacturing or retailing, grew rapidly in suburban and peripheral areas.

With the growth of urban freeway systems in the 1960s and continued use of the car, the frictionless zone expanded rather considerably, so that distance decay could only be observed at rather remarkable distances. Transport geographers and planners attempting to predict commuter trips from residential zones to workplace districts employed 'random coupling' models, as mobility had reached such a stage that there seemed no rhyme nor reason for home location to be associated with work location, at least in the extensive frictionless zone. As a result, not only could developers build homes over an ever-widening area, including non-metropolitan areas, but entrepreneurs were equally free to locate their offices and facilities virtually wherever they wished. The further result was an extremely low density population; an unplanned, uncoordinated series of commercial, service and manufacturing sites throughout the metropolitan area; and a general exodus of the more mobile white population out of the older inner cities into suburban and peripheral locations, leaving a growing black population residing in the inner cities.

With a relative decline of the C.B.D., work trips, which had focussed directionally on the downtown, began to take on 'lateral' characteristics. Trips were neither dominantly downtown nor toward the periphery but would fan out in all directions. With continued decentralization of activities, 'reverse' work trips, toward the periphery, became more common. There have also been increases in cross-town travel, more important in smaller urban areas but also common in large metropolitan areas with ring roads. These trips cross through or go around the congested C.B.D. The geometric simplicity of the early travel patterns has been replaced by a confusing complexity resulting from the spread of people and activities throughout metropolitan space, made possible by the reduction in the friction of distance.

Different socio-economic and racial groups participate differently in C.B.D. trips, lateral commuting, reverse work trips, and crosstown travel. The most notable departure from 'typical' commuting patterns is for black workers. Because of discrimination in the housing market and the preponderance

of both low income housing and public housing in the older
parts of the inner city, blacks have a more limited geographical choice of residence. However, employment, particularly
manual jobs, has been moving out of the inner city into suburban and peripheral areas. The result is that more blacks are
chasing fewer manual jobs further from where they live and
engaging in rather widespread reverse commuting. Some of
the longest commuter trips are undertaken by those who have
the least to spend on transport. On the other hand, profes-
sional and managerial workers, occupations having the highest incomes, will be involved in typically very long or very
short work trips. This situation results from the suburban and
peripheral residential locations of these workers and the suburban or peripheral location of workplace, 'short trips,' or
C.B.D. workplace location, 'long trips.'

The late 1970s have seen a slight upturn in the number of
passengers using some form of transit and a reversal of the
long-term decline in commuter transport. This modest increase in commuter passengers probably results from federal
policies toward transit and the increase in the cost of petrol.
Almost all federal transport policies in the past favoured the
automobile at the expense of commuter transport. No doubt
the greatest federal impact was the massive subsidies for
highway construction, including the 67,000 kilometres of the
limited access, multiple-lane interstate system. Even federal
housing policy, which favoured single-family dwellings, gave
indirect benefits to the automobile. In contrast, federal programmes emphasizing mass transit have been more recent
and clearly of more limited impact. A basic problem is that
political support for federal transport investment or subsidies
for transit is rather weak, since the electorate would be
greatly inconvenienced by a de-emphasis of the automobile.

The increases in the cost of petrol have led to quite a different future outlook for metropolitan areas. Increasing petrol prices may lead to the development of mass transit systems, which in turn will lead to more efficient rearrangement
of urban land uses and a more effective metropolitan spatial
structure. Environmental costs will be reduced, and the scat-

ter of people and activities will be altered into a more logical pattern. Another, quite different, scenario is that any significant increase in the number of commuters is not feasible from a cost point of view, as the automobile has created a de-concentrated metropolitan area that cannot be served by commuter transport. Instead, the emphasis should be placed on environmental improvements in the energy-efficient automobile, since the forces of deconcentration are simply too strong to stem. No doubt both these scenarios represent extreme points of view. However, the automobile has such a strong foothold on the commuting habits of Americans that the second scenario seems more realistic, at least in the short-term. The modest increases in commuting during the past few years were achieved with significant increases in operating costs. With escalating costs, it is not clear whether future increases in commuting can be sustained. Commuter services, depending on public funds, can probably not expect an ever larger share of limited public resources when commuter trips make up only a small portion of metropolitan travel.

AUTOS AND MASS TRANSIT[2]

Thirty centuries ago Solomon wrote "Where there is no vision the people perish" (Prov. 29:18). This is true now as it was then. Its corollary, "where there is vision the people prosper," of vital concern to everyone inherently implies the existence of a single, unified objective to guide society. The invention of the automobile has raised doubts about this.

In transportation today, there are at least two major, conflicting concepts of what future transportation goals ought to be. Automobile manufacturers, highway construction interests and oil companies together with what is probably a majority of the public equate paradise with private automobile

[2] Reprint of speech delivered by Daphne Christensen, science advisor to the Chicago Transit Authority, at Iowa State University on October 4, 1976. *Vital Speeches of the Day.* 43:77–81. N. 15, '76. Reprinted with permission.

ownership and see luxury on wheels and total mobility as the main societal goal. By contrast, the vision of transportation and land use planners, environmentalists, conservationists, and such diverse groups as downtown businessmen and welfare recipients, includes a significant role for public transportation so as to balance the proliferation of the automobile, and includes coaxing a larger percentage of the public into at least partial use of mass transit.

Confusion abounds because of the invisible interconnectedness of almost everything that happens today, making it difficult to relate cause and event. It is not possible to understand any one sequence of events concerning the major forces at work in the nation without consideration of secondary, feedback effects. Pollution, congestion, energy scarcity and unemployment are not separate afflictions. Consequently, proponents of one solution become opponents of others. The society as a whole becomes increasingly polarized and transportation is a prime example where auto and transit advocates make up opposite ends of the transportation spectrum.

And things are happening very fast. Motoring costs are soaring. The average vehicle on the road last year cost 23.5 cents a mile, up from 14.7 cents two years ago, according to the Hertz Corp., where the increase comes mainly from higher capital cost and increased depreciation and not from rising fuel prices. This observation conceals the fact that the immense demand for Arab oil, and the attendant dollar flow, recycled through Europe and back into this country account for a significant part of the inflationary/unemployment spiral. Economists have come to call this the "invisible" crisis. Clearly the automobile, through its energy consumption, creates its own inflation, something that didn't happen during the era of cheap oil. Things aren't what they used to be.

Many thinking people agree that since the automobile consumes over 60 percent of the oil used in this country, and the journey-to-work accounts for more than half of this, one intelligent approach toward energy self-sufficiency is to develop efficient public transit systems for at least work trips. Yet the moment a significant shift in auto use is proposed, the automobile industry feels threatened. Because the automobile sits at the center of our economy, with one in six employed in auto related jobs, the national economy is naturally sensitive to any shift in auto production.

Consequently, the thought of increased public transit usage produces an over-reaction in the auto industry. One of the most striking examples was what happened when Congress was considering an energy tax on large cars, to promote use of more efficient (and less profitable) smaller cars and as a means of producing revenue to finance greater efficiency in transportation. On April 29, 1975, T. A. Murphy, Chairman of General Motors, wrote to Congressman Al Ullman, Chairman of the House Ways and Means Committee, saying that of the 100,000 employees employed in large car production (a $3 billion investment to GM), "many would be out of work immediately and intense hardship could fall on them and the communities in which they reside." All considerations for big car tax were dropped.

Admittedly, threats of potential unemployment in the auto industry are potential threats to other areas. The Nobel Prize economist, Wassily Leontief, estimated that a $1 billion decline in sales (250,000 fewer cars), produced a loss of 57,900 jobs with 24,100 of these not directly related to auto vehicle production but in associated industries. Clearly if less cars were sold because they were used less and lasted longer, then some counteraction would be necessary to prevent hardship. In 1974, for example, sales of new autos dipped 23 percent below the previous year and 25 percent of the auto industry's 700,000 hourly workers were laid off. Yet if any progress is to be made in moving toward energy efficient living, some type of trade off must be made and adjustments must take place within the society. Uncertainty and inaction are not surprising in this tangled knot of problems and not just by citizens either; legislators, invested interests of each sector, administrators, and the separate specialists contribute to the stagnation and paralysis of remedial action.

It ought to be possible to ask what probable ends are served by various particular means. In this, the most powerful and technically advanced society in human history, we ought to be able to anticipate likely happenings from selected courses of actions, assess difficulties and compute ways to achieve a reasonable future. Planners like to quote Columbus as not just sailing, but as sailing west as an example that proper direction can make all the difference. Unfortunately, transportation has so many more dimensions other than scalor orientation that well-informed choices become more complex than might appear.

One curious result of this inherent complexity is the maze of different kinds of planning organizations which almost any community exhibits. Some of these organizations are civic groups, not empowered to implement or receive government grants; some are comprehensive, long range planning groups; some may be special state agencies dating from the 1950s under state funds. Other state agencies are funded for planning through the Highway Trust Fund, some are certified by the Office of Business and Management (OMB) to receive government funds, others are certified by the Urban Mass Transit Administration (UMTA) to receive their funds; some have special jurisdiction when interstate boundaries are involved; a few have authority to implement actions such as restrict auto use on streets or construct capital investments, such as county or municipal organization directly responsible to the taxpayers.

Although Chicago and New York began transportation planning early in the first part of the century, most other regions were less active until direct federal funding became available. The first highway planning funds came from the Hayden-Cartwright Act of 1935, and these were administered by the state highway groups which had been set up by the first Federal Aid Highway Act in 1916. In the early 1950s, two major state groups, the Chicago Area Transit Study (CATS) and the Penn-Jersey region put out the first modern comprehensive planning documents for metropolitan areas; the CATS document is often called the bible for urban areas. Mass transit planning as a federally supported activity began under the Housing Act of 1961 under HUD and in the following year by the Federal Aid Highway Act of 1962 under the Department of Commerce and later the Department of Transportation. Each agency had different sets of requirements and guidelines and each certified different local groups. With the passage of the UMTA legislation in 1964 a third set of guidelines, requirements and certified groups came into being.

About this time, the federal government began favoring regions for grants that had overall planning councils, and socalled HUD "701" funds were provided to set up such groups. By 1970, there were 476 such organizations nationally. This does not include independent local or state planning councils. In 1970, 80 percent of regional planning councils adopted transportation policies and plans but only 37 percent were recognized by the Department of Transportation. By 1973, 42 percent of organizations recognized by the Federal Highway Administration to do urban planning were still state agencies usually as called Section 134 agencies named for the section of legislation funding them; another 37 percent were councils directed by local officials and 17 percent were miscellaneous county and city organizations. Consequently, 1974 legislation demanded that funds pass through state groups to local groups in order that planning could take place in the urban area affected.

State governments were naturally reluctant to give up the power and influence that come with large federal funding; about 17 percent of metropolitan planning is still done by state agencies. In small states such as Maryland, Massachusetts, New Jersey and Connecticut it may be reasonable and according to tradition. In both Baltimore and Boston for example, state agencies carry out metropolitan planning. Considering that Alaska, the largest state, is 483 times the size of Rhode Island, the smallest state, it is extremely difficult for the federal government to develop guidelines which apply equally well to all situations, especially when it is noted that 38 metropolitan areas involving 2/3 of the states cross state boundaries.

These competing agencies frequently have overlapping

and indistinct responsibilities; many to believe that if we could just straighten out these administrative problems, urban transportation would be greatly assisted. Not necessarily true! Although the planning process, especially that of complying with federal requirements for funds *may be awkward and clumsy, it does for the most part work* in so far as it goes with a variety of practical working mechanisms such as ad hoc task forces promoting communication and understanding. The real reason that planning groups cannot for example deal more effectively with constraints on the automobile is not for lack of power. Admittedly, the Regional Transportation Authority of Northeastern Illinois (RTA) is one of the few such regional agencies which has this specific power. The RTA does have the undisputed authority to block off traffic and ban automobiles anywhere. But no responsible agency would ban automobiles without a suitable alternative. And any agency that did take such action would not last through the next election. Efforts to improve and clarify planning are commendable but there is danger that attention to improving the organizations detracts from the real task at hand, that of building a suitable ground transportation system.

Thus, entirely too much emphasis has come to be placed on the planning network itself and attendant problems and the focus removed from the original purpose.

Transportation planning, as practiced today, is therefore primarily confined to purely local mobility land use interaction and interfacing with the federal government. In most cases, progress at the local or regional level is hampered by the strong urban/suburban polarization which exists in almost every metropolitan area. Thus it is unlikely that the kind of imaginative concepts needed to alleviate the auto-transit confrontation will arise from traditional transportation planning as it has evolved.

Further, it is probably unreasonable to expect much from either of the automobile orientated or transit industries since both involve people who feel obligated to represent the short-term interests of a given community. In principle, if not in fact, the responsibility for national problem resolution rests with the federal government, although historically this is not evident in transportation policy.

Traditionally, any change in transit policy has only come about through some kind of crisis, either a war or labor unrest, or whatever, and then, once some solution was enacted, it was copied again and again even though the circumstances of later situations may have been entirely different. Each transit mode, whether rail, air or surface was always treated independently without thought of impact on the others. This has gone on for nearly 100 years.

So ubiquitous has the automobile become that we are apt to forget that through the first part of this century, rails dominated transportation, even holding up well through the Depression. Early transportation policy, to the extent that such policy can be said to exist, was regulatory in nature and aimed at curbing excesses in rail practices. At the start of this century, roads were considered a rural matter and handled by the Office of Road Inquiry in the Department of Agriculture. The first federal legislation came in 1916 when the government financed 50 percent of road construction but managed to do so only over the strong objection of many states that had invested in their own roads and didn't consider this area fitting for federal intervention. After 1956, the federal government began financing 90 percent of road highway construction and since 1956 has invested over $76 billion in what surely must be the largest public works project in the history of the world.

When the 1956 Federal-Aid Highway Act was passed, there were those who warned of the probable outcome. The perceptive critic Lewis Mumford saw what he termed "the fatal mistake in sacrificing every form of transportation to the private automobile"; he said the most charitable assumption was that Congress had not the faintest notion what it was doing in this "ill-conceived, ill-balancing of transportation." He prophesied many of the seeming irreversible dilemmas facing us today.

Much of the legislation which has had a devastating impact on unbalancing the transportation system was undertaken (pun intended!) without any awareness on anyone's part of its future impact. For example, in 1934, the Federal Housing Authority (FHA) was formed to stimulate employment in the building industry, and offset the effects of the Depression. Within 40 years, the FHA alone insured over 182 billion aiding 50 million households; the success of this program led to other similar investments creating the immense urban sprawl of low density housing, inefficient and costly to maintain, and geared to automobile use.

Another example of early legislation punitive to transit was the Holding Act of 1935 which made it mandatory for all utility companies to divest themselves of interest in transit, in the belief that transit received an unfair advantage. No one understood that public transit is an integral and important part of the ground transportation system, and necessary for national prosperity but instead treated transit as a competitor to the automobile. Thus legislation was taken which purposely harmed transit, while the federal government promoted complete dependence on the automobile almost without realizing it.

The recognition of the role of public transit as a necessary part of the nation's total transportation system did not come until the early 1960s, first as a needed social force, under the Housing Act of 1961 and next under the Urban Mass Transit Act of 1964. At first, only emergency-type funds were provided for existing transit systems in danger of collapse in the way of loans, capital grants and studies. This permitted cities to purchase private companies near bankruptcy and maintain some semblance of service. The Urban Mass Transportation Administration (UMTA) performed an admirable job: today 333 transit companies are publicly owned (35 percent) and carry 90 percent of all passengers over 86 percent of the miles; many private small bus companies still exist, as in New Jersey which has 165 companies each with one bus. UMTA has also performed well in sprinkling a generous supply of buses about the nation, and helping to refurbish antiquated systems. Professor Alan Altshuler of MIT recently observed that in view of the efforts required in 1963 and 1964 to secure passage of a minimal transit capital investment act, "the rapid growth in aid over the past eleven years could not have been imagined."

But much of this growth in support has not been due to UMTA but in spite of it. In 1974, transit operators reached another crisis when operating costs exceeded income by about $350 million; it was known that raising fares would not only cause a hardship to those least able to afford it, but in addition that a fare increase would only result in a ridership decline, resulting in greater use of the automobile and in some cases less total revenue. Attempts to get UMTA's assistance in requesting federal funds fell on deaf ears. In desperation, city officials, through the U.S. Conference of Mayors formed an ad hoc task force consisting of city officials, transit representatives and interested parties including Mr. Henry Ford of the Ford Motor Company, and arranged a meeting, without the support of the Secretary of Transportation, with President Ford. It was shown that a raise in fares to meet this deficit would stimulate an increase in the economic index which in turn would mean that the purchases made by the U.S. Government in normal government business would cost an additional $500 million. It was therefore cheaper for the government to assist in maintaining fares than to allow such fares to rise driving inflation. Within days an operating subsidy bill was passed by Congress and this came within weeks of statements by UMTA administrators that operating subsidies would never be passed.

But achieving things through legislation alone can be an exasperatingly slow process. Nor is legislation alone sufficient; much depends on how it is administered and it is not unusual in federal programs to have the administering of a program undermine the legislative intent, even though it may not always be purposeful.

One of the most striking examples of this was in the case of the Boston Restudy. Between 1971 and 1973, following a citizen's revolt against further freeway expansion, an 18 month study deleted several planned highway projects, opting instead for a transit development to be funded using the Highway Trust Funds as permitted under recent hard-won "Bust the Trust" legislation. Yet when Boston submitted the paper work for the transfer of funds, their environmental impact statement was rejected by UMTA. This brought cries of alarm since a previous environmental impact statement showing the area could withstand the ravages of a super highway had already previously been approved by the Highway Administration. Surely by any common sense, any small transit system would be less destructive. Nevertheless, UMTA declined to accept any of the drafts prepared by Boston, judging them inadequate for one or another reason. Such a decision caused months of unnecessary delay and did not help increase the respect for transit officials by Boston taxpayers.

This points to one of the key problems in dealing with the vast government bureaucracy: local officials are directly responsible to the electorate and the government federal administrators are not. What happens then can best be explained by a typical event that happened in Denver. Within days after the voters approved the formation of their regional organization, and voted matching funds for government grants, Denver submitted a capital grant application for 93 buses. For an entire year, nothing was heard. Then UMTA approved the application without any explanation whatever for the long delay. Considering that it takes another one–two years to receive the buses after the purchase order is presented, the Denver officials were certainly hard pressed to maintain voter support over such a long period of time with no results to show.

Another happier example happened just a year ago in Washington, D.C., where Metro construction was halted because of lack of funds. UMTA recommended use of a newly devised policy of building systems in incremental stages when funds ran low, putting small portions into service over a stretched-out period. Transit officials noted that it would delay the system four years, cost an additional $500 million, and invite voter wrath. Within a week after this decision was reported, UMTA issued a statement that highway funds would be transferred to complete the system. Evidently, UMTA can be sensitive to citizen response when it is in their own backyard. Many around the country wish this marvelous display of care and concern could be extended to those areas not under the nose of the capital building.

Time and again we see that what constitutes a reasonable "intuitive conclusion" in the offices of a vast bureaucracy is very different than at the local level. In a letter dated February 6, 1974 to the Senate Appropriations Committee Chairman, Senators Clifford Case and Robert Byrd advised the Congress to not accept intuitive judgment on the part of Department of Transportation, in matters of such cost and complexity as new transit systems. Those who framed the Constitution would be shocked to learn that intuitive judgment contradicting local views would ever be considered by anyone, and were it not for the fact that the federal bureaucracy is the only source of funds, these intuitive views would surely never be considered at all. Certainly the transit industry often feels that the significant attempts to rebalance the transit system of this country are not always materially aided by the practices which the bureaucracy often invokes.

Taking a broader view, it may be asking the impossible that the Department of Transportation deal equitably with auto and transit interests alike, just judging from the vast differences in makeup of the two communities. The automobile industry must surely rank as one of the all time glamour and growth industries of our time: the leadership alone is impressive: two-thirds of the top 15 companies in each year's ranking of the largest industrial companies are either automobile companies or allied industries in oil and steel. Further, the automobile industry is the major purchaser from about 50,000 other smaller companies. The labor unions are among the largest and well known. Union leader's names are household words and some are said to be "union statesmen." Vast sums of money flow in all directions, toward enormous advertising expenditures and toward political campaigns especially in what makes up the highway lobby. Many legislators at the federal level have said they would like to vote for urban transit but are prevented in doing so because of the pervasive highway lobby. Even at the state level, the force and influence of highway money is formidable; they are able to command headlines to defeat even small appropriations for public transit, and contributions for political campaigns in Illinois alone run to six figures. Such awesome power commands attention and respect and it is little wonder that the federal administrative bureaucracy gives them special treatment.

Contrast this against the management situation in mass transit. A recent study by Marquette University emphasized that almost no other industry has been as hard pressed to attract, develop and train qualified managerial talent since qualified people move to more attractive growth industries. Advancement and promotion have been slow with economy the key issue and this has been going on for almost 30 years. The scars of austerity in attempting to run a system in view of rising costs and declining income have brought about a kind of stagnation and unwillingness to risk change, or even to see the need for change; many areas of modern technology, commonly applied in other industries, are still largely unfamiliar to transit managers. Some have estimated that only the top 10–12 percent of the transit industry management is really qualified to understand and respond to much of what concerns federal administrators. Conversely, the federal government bureaucracy has little inclination to take such action as say, hiring a bus garage superintendent with 30 years experience to read and translate federal guidelines and regulations to be understandable to other bus garage superintendents. In Chicago, we have an excellent management training institute but it is rare among transit organizations. Terrell Hill, a well-known transit executive summed it up recently by saying: "We're boiling water when we should be milking a cow." It isn't hard to understand why UMTA and transit are often at loggerheads.

Things are changing of course. More colleges are turning out good students who see transit imbalance as a challenge and support the need of better public systems, if not always support of existing systems. And society as a whole is changing. Some of the youth movement of the 1960s that rejected materialism seems to have taken root. People talk more about the need for a happier, more fulfilling life and there is less talk about longer automobiles and thinner television sets. A significant part of the population still spend large sums of money for the latest in automotive status symbols while neglecting their children's teeth, but there is also the growing voice of conservationists and environmentalists, for an improved balance between the individual and the environment. Today, the majority of households have at least one person with some college education and simplistic views no longer control national direction as they once did.

Conscience is said to pose problems and power solves them. The transit industry alone does not have sufficient power to solve the problems facing the nation as a whole. Until now, there has been a shaky coalition between transit and urban interests, conservationists and environmentalists and the like trying to make progress against the awesome power of the automobile and oil industries. In a nation where there are more licensed drivers than voters, it has been an uphill struggle, with but modest gains and in the face of continual erosion. Yet today we see the automobile industry putting out bids for studies on better traffic control implying that some constraints on the auto can be tolerated. We see auto executives attending meetings concerned with the interests of transit; we see auto company employees in technology assessment seminars, and, according to the recent Marquette University Study, we see older transit organizations such as Chicago's, making a determined effort, with some success, to bring enlightened management to transit industry. It may be fair to say that the nation's collective conscience is becoming evident. Never a captive of logic, federal transportation policy is moving toward building reasonably balanced systems. Considering the vast potential of this nation for accomplishment, these may be enough.

Those regions that solve their transportation problems will survive and prosper; it can mean a brighter future for ourselves, our children and grandchildren. We must all work together to find new solutions, to show what a strong and vital people can accomplish.

HOW CITIES ARE COAXING PEOPLE
OUT OF THEIR CARS[3]

Through bold ideas and dogged promotion, a group of cities across the country is trying to prove that mass transit can be an attractive and practical alternative to the automobile.

For motorists weary of rush-hour anxieties and expensive gasoline, buses and trolleys in these communities now possess an allure they have not displayed before.

For civic leaders in such places, public transportation today is seen not just as a costly service, but as a way to ease traffic jams, improve air quality and possibly even revitalize decaying neighborhoods.

New enthusiasm is evident in the variety of innovative schemes being devised, ranging from transit malls and personalized dial-a-ride services to trolley and rail systems. Coming at a time when gasoline costs $1 a gallon and more, the innovations and improvements appear to be having the desired effect.

Public transit almost everywhere is more popular these days. Ridership in 1979 on the nation's public-transit systems is up by 5 percent. But some cities are taking special steps to enhance the attractiveness of mass transit.

Following is a closer look at what seven cities are doing to coax motorists aboard buses, trolleys and trains.

Portland, Oreg.

Portland transit officials adopted a simple and successful formula—cheap fares and frequent bus service—to encourage drivers to leave their cars at home.

Since 1978, fares have stayed at 45 to 65 cents—the exact amount depends on the distance traveled. What's more, in a

[3] Reprint of staff-written article. *U.S. News & World Report.* 87:38–40. D. 24, '79.
Copyright 1979, U.S. News & World Report, Inc.

300-block area in the city's center, dubbed "fareless square," passengers ride free.

Bus service improved significantly after the development of a 22-block transit mall in the city's commercial and retail core. Built in 1977, the 16-million-dollar mall is designed for use mainly by pedestrians and buses. Car access is limited. Special lanes restricted to buses have reduced congestion, and trips between Portland's suburbs and downtown now are 15 minutes shorter.

As a result, bus ridership is 125 percent greater than in 1973, while auto traffic has declined to 1971-72 levels.

There are positive side effects, too. Carbon-monoxide emissions in the downtown area have decreased by 22 percent in the last five years, and pedestrians are able to benefit from shelters, kiosks, sculpture and other art as well as parks added to the mall area.

A once-moribund center city is taking on new vitality. J.C. Penney canceled plans to move out of the downtown area. A new 150,000-square-foot department store was opened by Nordstrom in 1976. One million more square feet of space is under construction.

The mall's success is spurring Portland to build a 15-mile "light rail" line—akin to the trolley lines of times past and far cheaper to erect than conventional subways—from downtown Portland to its principal suburb, Gresham. The 162-million-dollar system should be completed by 1985.

Seattle

In the past six years, city leaders gambled 120 million dollars that Seattle residents could be lured out of their cars and onto the public buses.

One-hundred-fifty buses that fold in the middle and can carry 108 passengers—30 more than a conventional bus—are now in operation. The 52-mile trackless-trolley system that meanders through the city has been rebuilt. Fourteen park-and-ride lots have been set up on the city's perimeter to make it easier for suburban residents to use the bus. A free-ride zone was created in the heart of town.

To make residents aware of the changes, the city spent $225,000 last year for advertising in newspapers, on the radio and on billboards.

Seattle has also won business support for employer-subsidized monthly commuter passes. In October, the state's largest bank, Seattle First, decided to underwrite the cost of bus commuting for 3,800 employes. This year's tab is $500,000.

The gamble seems to have paid off. Ridership has doubled since 1973. Almost half the people making their way to downtown Seattle in the morning rush hour travel by bus.

Now, however, transit officials face a new problem. Explains Neil Peterson, executive director of Seattle's Metro: "We no longer have to sell people on using buses. Our problem now is meeting demand."

Minneapolis-St. Paul

Like its counterpart in Seattle, the Twin Cities Metropolitan Transit Commission is now grappling with the results of its own success.

Discount fares and reliable service lured so many area residents to buses that the MTC must use its advertising budget to mollify riders who can't get seats on crowded buses during rush hours.

Every Monday since late September, the MTC has added four to six refurbished buses to the fleet, which as of early December numbered more than 850. Even so, demand for seats isn't being met. In the past year, ridership has increased by 7.8 percent, from a daily average of 255,000 trips to 275,000.

One reason for the increase is a 4-month-old program that permits area employers to sell monthly bus passes to their workers at a 12.5 percent discount through payroll deduction. Passes purchased from an employer cost only $14—$2 less than the regular price—and some companies make them available for just $10. So far, 3,000 people are taking advantage of this payroll plan to purchase their passes, and another

2,000 are expected to be enrolled in the program by early next year.

The MTC also offers unlimited rides on weekends for $1. This program got off to a slow start in 1977, but caught on last summer during the gasoline crunch. In July, 18,500 passengers bought weekend passes—a 95 percent increase over the same month in 1978.

San Mateo, Calif.

Once tagged a public-transportation wasteland, Northern California's San Mateo County is now setting records in mass transit. Bus ridership totals 68,000 passengers a day—almost five times the 1976 level.

The increase is particularly notable because only 18 million dollars has been invested in four years to develop a countywide public-transit system almost from scratch.

Instead of buying new $125,000 buses, the county bought used diesel buses and fixed them up for about $15,000 apiece.

"We've tried to make public transit a bargain," explains John Mauro, general manager of the San Mateo County Transit District. Mauro and other transit officials attribute much of the system's success to a decision to let private operators provide the service where it is deemed appropriate. For instance, Sam Trans, as the San Mateo County Transit District is known, buys blocks of tickets on Southern Pacific Railroad commuter trains bound for San Francisco and resells them at a discount of 30 percent to the county's commuters.

Greyhound provides service on six north-south trunk routes between Palo Alto and San Francisco. A private contractor is paid $396,000 a year to offer dial-a-ride service for the elderly and handicapped.

Routes are monitored and reviewed regularly and changed to improve service to major destinations such as San Francisco's International Airport, where more than 14,000 of the county's 555,000 residents work.

Given their success so far, transit officials are projecting a steady yearly growth of 10 to 15 percent in the next five years.

Syracuse, N.Y.

In this upstate New York city, the elderly and disabled enjoy a transit luxury that several other cities are just starting to offer: Personalized door-to-door service known as Call-a-Bus.

The program, begun as a federally sponsored experiment five years ago, is being labeled a success. In fact, it has become so popular that overcrowding now occurs.

Riders must give dispatchers seven days' advance notice of when they want to be picked up; when the program first began, a two-day lead time was adequate. Even with this stricter advance-notice requirement, demand is still so high that officials have been forced to set priorities. Those passengers needing medical transportation get first call. Riders on a personal business trip may have to wait.

Run by the Central New York Transportation Authority, Call-a-Bus costs $300,000 a year to operate. Seven days a week, from 6 A.M. to 10 P.M., one large bus and four cheerfully painted minibuses—all equipped for wheelchairs—carry passengers across Onondaga County.

Each passenger must pay 50 cents or $1 each way, depending on the distance traveled. Monthly volume averages about 5,000 passengers, including more than 700 wheelchair riders.

Denver

Officials here are convinced that a 53-million-dollar transit plaza and a billion-dollar light-rail system can relieve auto congestion and reduce the brown haze that envelops the area.

Next February, the city will close one of its busiest arteries, 16th Street, and turn it into a 14-block plaza for buses and pedestrians. By late 1981, the noisy cars and smelly fumes will be replaced by trees, 20-foot-wide brick sidewalks, colorful pedestrian shelters and a fleet of 17 buses that will shuttle people back and forth for free. During rush hour, these buses will run every 70 seconds.

At each end of the mall, there will be turnaround transit centers where passengers can transfer to buses bound for out-lying areas. No longer forced to spend the bulk of the rush hour fighting downtown traffic, bus drivers will be able to make twice as many trips to the city's center.

To reduce congestion even more, city officials want state approval to build a 73-mile light-rail system from central Denver to 15 miles outside the city in every direction.

As proposed, the system would be paid for from tax revenues of the six counties it would serve. "We'd welcome federal assistance," says Richard C. Thomas, chairman pro tem of the Regional Transportation Board of directors, "but, frankly, we can't wait. That's why we're going to our State Legislature." The proposal will be submitted to the Legislature in January, but probably won't come to a vote until spring. Officials say the outlook for approval is "too close to call."

Nashville

Following the same sophisticated advertising techniques that auto companies use, city transit officials three years ago began a marketing campaign to attract motorists to the bus.

Using a $937,000 federal grant, the Metropolitan Transit Authority ran frequent TV, radio and newspaper advertisements stressing Nashville's economy car, the local bus. One television ad was almost identical to an auto commercial. A draped vehicle was shown in front of the city's replica of the Parthenon. As the sun broke on the horizon and clouds drifted by, a voice announced that Nashville's new economy car was about to be unveiled. The cloth was removed to reveal a white and royal-blue city bus.

New routes and an improved telephone information system followed the advertising campaign and in one year, ridership increased from 7 million passengers to 7.8 million.

These days, the ads are played less frequently but ridership has reached 8.7 million.

NO FREE RIDE FOR U.S. MASS TRANSIT MANUFACTURERS[4]

It was called the "Transit Renaissance." Heralded as an answer to urban traffic congestion, to automobile exhaust pollution and to overdependence on gasoline energy, it would encourage modernization of existing transit systems and foster and finance new ones. Importantly, it also promised reinvigoration of the American transit car building business and the bus business. For industries whose decline had been marked and whose future had been dim, it offered new prospects for profits, for growth and for jobs.

The "Transit Renaissance" was born of the massive government financial assistance to mass transportation—funds from federal, state and local sources. Federal funding which began as modest planning monies in 1961 was greatly expanded with the initiation of the capital grant program in 1964 and the operating subsidy program in 1974. Although mass transit funding never approached federal highway funding, it did provide from 1965 to 1980 some $10 billion for rail capital projects, among them rights-of-way, equipment and operation. Approximately $1.75 billion of this was spent on railcars.

The successes of the program include the new transit rail systems of Washington, D.C. and Atlanta, major assistance to San Francisco (for "BART"—the Bay Area Rapid Transit) and the modernization and extension of lines in Boston, Philadelphia, Chicago and New York. New systems are being built now in Baltimore, Miami and Buffalo.

While numbers of the rail transit systems are having serious problems today, their problems would indisputably be far greater indeed without the governmental aid programs. Similarly, the nation's urban transit operators have been able to

[4] Article by William J. Ronan, former MTA chairman. *Journal of the Institute for Socioeconomic Studies.* VI, 2:24–37. Summer '81. By permission of the Institute for Socioeconomic Studies. All rights reserved.

expand their bus fleets and to modernize them on an unprecedented scale.

But what of the vista of earnings, profits and growth that the program offered American transit car builders and motor bus manufacturers? For the former, the great and expected "shot-in-the-arm" proved more toxic than therapeutic. For the latter, what should have been a bonanza proved more of a fiasco.

The Railcar Story

When the transit aid program began some 20 years ago, there were three American companies that built self-propelled electric railcars: The St. Louis Car Company (a division of General Steel Industries), The Pullman-Standard Company and The Budd Company. Today, two of them are out of the business—St. Louis and Pullman-Standard (except for finishing certain commitments)—and the third, Budd, has reentered the business after leaving it, but is now German-owned.

During this period, three major American companies, Rohr, Boeing and General Electric, also entered the car-building business. All of them have now withdrawn as prime contractors. Of the six, then, there now is only one—The Budd Company—and it is no longer American-owned.

Even though federal law requires that 51 percent of the components and/or labor of railcars purchased with any federal funding must be American, a look at the current list of manufacturers who take railcar bids reads like the roster of an international conclave:

Kawasaki (Japan)
Tokyu (Japan)
Franco-Belge (Belgium)
Siemens-Duwag (Germany)
Breda (Italy)
Hawker Siddeley (Canada)
Bombardier (Canada)
Canadian Vickers (Canada)
Budd (U.S.A., German-owned)

Why was so promising a potential for American car builders not realized? Why did transit systems and the car builders
have such difficulties? The causes are multiple; the answers
several.

The Traditional Car Building Industry

The traditional car builders were principally assemblers.
The St. Louis firm, as a part of General Steel Industries, did
furnish cast trucks and Budd did furnish fabricated trucks. All
builders furnished the car body, but got the bulk of the components from other companies—wheels, couplers, compres-
sors, doors, motors, controllers, heaters, air-conditioners, etc.

The traditional pattern led to difficulties for the car
builder when transit operators in the spirit of the Transit Renaissance began to specify longer warranties and new, more
sophisticated components for the cars. Assembly, heretofore,
had not been that different from one order to another. Now,
with the onset of electronic devices and other innovations,
"systems engineering" to concert the operation of car components taxed the knowledge and capacities of the car builders.

At this juncture, also, the transit agencies began not just
legally but in practice to hold the car builder responsible for
the whole car—making him warrant for a longer time the entire vehicle—components and all. The Metropolitan Transportation Authority in New York led in this move. The aim
was to ensure that there was responsibility definitely fixed and
to preclude any shuffling of responsibility for unsatisfactory
results among the car builder and the various component
manufacturers.

Problems Followed Money

Before the government aid programs, orders for rail transit cars were neither very numerous nor very large. With the
advent of federal-state-local financing, larger orders were
placed and more orders were available for competitive bidding. The larger orders, obviously, should have provided an

opportunity for mass production methods in manufacture and a consequent saving in the unit cost per car. However, encountering design and production difficulties, the traditional car builders experienced long delays in delivery and increased costs. They found these problems further exacerbated by the late penalties which transit agencies insisted upon putting into contracts to ensure delivery in timely fashion. The riding public was impatient for the new equipment it had been promised.

Long delays had the further effect, of course, of intensifying the damage done both supplier and customer by inflation. Fixed price contracts became ruinous to many manufacturers whose deliveries and ensuing payments were months or years behind schedule.

The traditional car builders had also been accustomed to manufacturing according to detailed specifications for virtually every segment of the car. In an industry that had not progressed significantly in technology, these specifications were not drastically altered from one car order to another. When the new transit systems, and also the existing systems, undertook to shift to "performance specifications," the car builder was accorded more discretion on the hardware, but became responsible for its performance. This new status for the car builder conferred, as it developed, a considerable risk for him.

Trouble with New Cars

The M-1 Long Island Railroad "new generation" commuter cars required faster acceleration and braking than earlier cars. Stops and starts also had to be smoother. The Budd Company encountered great difficulty meeting these requirements. The first M-1s experienced uncalled-for setting of brakes. Restarting motors also proved troublesome after power was cut in and out on the third rail power system's gaps. Budd had to bring in consulting electrical engineers as well as General Electric and WABCO to solve the problems. Accomplishing the necessary corrective retrofit ultimately required nothing less than construction of a new Budd facility at Flushing Meadows Park in New York. It had become apparent—a very expensive realization—that the work could not be done at Budd's own plant near Philadelphia.

The weight of transit cars had become a matter of concern to transit operators, particularly as air-conditioning, insulation and advanced control mechanisms were added. Weights threatened to exceed maximum tolerances for the structures on which the cars would operate. Another caution was that heavier cars meant more power consumption to run them. Weight limitations were accordingly inserted into contracts and, in order to assure reasonable compliance, penalties for excess weight were called for. The builder's problems were compounded. Weight-saving requirements added to his engineering tasks at the very time he was contending with the newer technology. Even requirements for aesthetic treatment of cars' interior and exterior appearance proved troublesome.

For their protection, transit operating agencies traditionally inserted into the car contracts a requirement that their "engineer" approve the drawings of the car and the progress of the car production through the builder's plant. The "engineer" was critical in the acceptance of the car as well. When detailed specifications were the order of the day, the "engineer's" involvement was a simpler matter than when "performance specifications" and new technological developments became current. Winning the "engineer's" approvals became more difficult and this added to costs.

Construction of the New Haven Railroad's new commuter cars, the M-2s, was a case in point. For one, the manufacturer found that the cars were attaining a heavier weight than anticipated. In addition, there was difficulty in meeting the performance specification for the braking system. That specification required that an all-air brake be a backup in the event of failure of dynamic braking. The backup caused trouble, creating excessive heat in the wheels of the cars. The "engineer's" insistence that the performance specifications be met led to a retrofit which included installation of a different quality of wheels.

Fate of Traditional Producers

For the traditional car builders, new large orders revealed that they were not really adequately prepared for the volume and complexities encountered. Nor did they only have to cope with one antagonist when dealing with these problems. They now were not only under the surveillance of their transit agency contractor, but also of the bureaucracies of the federal, state and local government agencies that were involved in the financing arrangements and whose approvals were required before payment could be made.

In fact, successfully bidding for contracts repeatedly proved to be pyrrhic victories for many of the major contractors. Thus, the St. Louis Car Company ran into difficulties with the large order for the R-44 subway car for the New York City Transit Authority. Its cost overruns due to delays, retrofits and penalties bordered on the catastrophic. It ceased bidding as a prime contractor after the losses it suffered. When Westinghouse bid unsuccessfully on the R-46 car with St. Louis as the car assembler, the latter firm left the business. Similarly, The Budd Company took the large order for the MTA of New York's Long Island Railroad cars, the M-1s, and its losses were such that it, too, bowed out for several years insofar as prime contracting was concerned. It continued to serve as a subcontractor and to build railroad trailer cars. Recently under its new ownership it has again bid as a prime contractor. The Pullman-Standard Company won the record order for more than 700 R-46 subway cars for New York. It ran into grave difficulties especially on the trucks for these cars which developed serious cracks in service. It recently lost a suit to the City of New York requiring the company to pay some $72 million and is now being sued for late delivery as well.

The Newcomers and How They Fared

The greater part of the value in a rail transit car is in components, viz. motors, trucks, controls, alternators, compres-

sors and the like. Inasmuch as General Electric and Westinghouse supply much of this equipment, they were urged by
transit agencies and others to enter the business as prime
contractors for transit cars. General Electric did so, beginning
by taking over from the Budd Company responsibility for the
additional M-1 commuter railcars for the Long Island and
Penn Central's Harlem and Hudson Divisions, all for the Metropolitan Transportation Authority of New York.

General Electric built a facility in Erie, Pennsylvania for
the assembling of cars and was the successful bidder on self-
propelled commuter railcars—the M-2s—for the MTA's New
Haven Division, the Southeastern Pennsylvania Transportation Authority in the Philadelphia area and the Erie-Lack-
awanna in the northern part of New Jersey. General Electric
was one of the two bidders on the difficult car specifications
set by the Metropolitan Atlanta Rapid Transit Authority. The
low bid, however, was from a foreign company, Franco-
Belge, which occasioned vigorous objections by General
Electric. Considering itself better qualified with a proven
record of quality production and seeing future prospects for
orders discouraging, General Electric thereupon withdrew as
a prime bidder and converted its new plant to locomotive
manufacture.

The "Transit Renaissance" was spurred by the bold futuristic BART system in the San Francisco area. Breaking with
the traditional systems, BART had its own gauge of track, automated operation, automatic ticketing and car design. No
system had ever started from scratch and moved into a new
technology—much untried in actual redundant operation—
in the rail rapid transit industry. It was not surprising, therefore, that the BART contract went to the Rohr Corporation,
an aerospace company that had the additional advantage of
being located in the state of California.

This was a time of great interest and excitement about the
potentialities of electronics, automation, new light materials,
and new standards of comfort for rail rapid transit. In London, the new Victoria Line of the Underground was automated. In Japan, the "Bullet Train" was a dramatic achieve-

ment. Elsewhere there were experiments in air cushion trains, magnetic levitation, linear induction motors and the like.

Aerospace Industry on Needy List

All of this coincided with U.S. aerospace cutbacks and a slowing down of the aviation industry. Indeed, it was at this point that Congress killed the American SST program, which analysts had thought would so significantly figure in aviation's future. Aerospace companies, in the doldrums and experiencing mounting unemployment, were seeking diversification. The Nixon Administration endeavored to help by encouraging them to enter the ground transportation field.

Of the aerospace firms, only the Rohr Corporation and Boeing actually entered the business as prime contract, successful railcar bidders. United Aircraft, Garrett, and LTV did, however, enter other phases. The experience of both the prime contract bidders was unfortunate. Its catastrophic experience with the BART order brought Rohr into serious financial straits. Boeing found its orders for light rail vehicles far more of a headache and costly than it had planned. The effort to apply aerospace production methods and technology proved more complex than anticipated. The urban transit environment was vastly different from air and space. Ironically, whereas the traditional car builders were equipped to handle the new technology, the aerospace industry lacked the specific experience necessary for dealing with the rigors of ground transportation. Both Rohr and Boeing have left the business as prime contractors for car building.

Foreign Entrance Into the Market

Successful low bids by foreign companies have taken a sizable share of the current market, largely by American default. With their European, Japanese and other "home" markets secure, many foreign suppliers are in a position to compete vigorously, even though 51 percent of the vehicle must be comprised of American parts or more than half built by

American labor. It is alleged by some American companies that many such foreign enterprises are subsidized by their governments and by lower wage rates, a story reminiscent of the complaints of the U.S. automobile industry. Entries on the other side of the ledger must also be acknowledged, however. No matter how inconclusive the results, the United States government, it should be noted, has subsidized a substantial amount of research and development for the American producers.

The Bus Story

The Federal Mass Transportation Program was a boon initially to the bus business. The increase in the demand for buses came not only with the availability of government funding, but also as a result of the public take-overs of the privately owned bus transit companies in most of the urban areas of the nation. This spread of public ownership was accelerated by the availability of federal funds for such acquisitions.

At the inception of the program, there were basically two companies in the bus business. The giant was General Motors. Flxible was its far smaller competitor. Both built what were called "New Look" buses. The soubriquet stemmed from the late 1950s when it was borrowed from the contemporaneous women's fashion offerings of Christian Dior. In the instance of buses, however, "New Look" did not indicate any radical departure from the appearance of the pre-World War II designs it succeeded.

As produced by the two companies, the buses were notable in both their similarity and serviceability. They had the special attraction of being "off-the-shelf" items readily available to practical purchasers.

Bus Prototype Developed

The appearance of new, "Transit Renaissance" financing inspired more demanding tastes, however. A new generation transit bus was deemed necessary. The industry worked on it through the American Public Transit Association bus development committee. General Motors, on its own, developed a prototype. At this juncture, the Urban Mass Transportation Administration of the U.S. Department of Transportation intervened. It wanted an advanced standard bus to be built. The availability of federal funding would be dependent upon attainment of the specifications DOT set for such a bus. A management consulting firm, with no special expertise in the motor bus field, was engaged to oversee and direct the federal effort.

The so-called "Transbus" was developed and three manufacturers, General Motors, Flxible and AM General, a newcomer to the field, built prototypes that were shown around the country. A second phase of this program—to build several hundred of such buses and put them in service in urban areas for extensive experience—never was carried through. Instead, the Urban Mass Transportation Administration settled on specifications for an "Advanced Design Bus" and both General Motors and Flxible undertook to build and market such vehicles, each with its own particular methods of meeting the federal specifications.

The new buses met with protests from many of the bus operators on the grounds of their costs, their "maintainability" and their weight. The bus picture was further complicated by a decision of the federal government to require all transit buses to be accessible to the handicapped, including wheelchair users. The interplay (which is a neutral word) among the parties resulted in confusion and frustration, with results bordering both on the ridiculous and chaotic. Several operators sought to acquire the traditional, so-called "New Look" bus, but this was no longer made in the United States. It could be ordered from General Motors, but only GM Canada which acquired it from General Motors U.S.A.

Here again the aerospace industry was to make an entry into the ground transit field which failed to fulfill many advance expectations. As part of its mass transportation venture, the Rohr Company acquired Flxible, but when the financial crisis hit Rohr, Flxible was sold to Grumman Corporation. The new method of framing and assembling buses introduced by Rohr accordingly became a Grumman responsibility. The rest is history. The development of structural cracks in the so-called "A" frame, and other difficulties resulted in Grumman buses being taken out of service in New York and several other major cities that had acquired them. The retrofit program by the company is now in progress. The General Motors advanced design bus has had some "bugs" but no major structural problems. In addition to the technical difficulties, public reaction to the new buses has by no means been overwhelmingly enthusiastic. The dark windows through which it is difficult to see at night impress many as a particularly dubious refinement. The sealed window frames of the Grumman version of the bus brought riders in torrid Houston to such a point of distraction that, when air-conditioning repeatedly broke down, they battered the windows open.

Foreign Bus Procurement

The total need for transit buses in the United States is such that General Motors, one manufacturer, could easily produce them all on a mass production basis. It has not therefore been a market to attract and hold newcomers from the United States. AM General entered the field but left soon afterward.

Several foreign manufacturers have, nonetheless, found a niche in the American market. They make more special vehicles, notably, the articulated bus and double-deck bus (particularly the former). The German MAN and Neoplan companies have won orders and the Hungarian Icarus has bid on some contract offerings.

There has also been an effort by New York Governor Hugh L. Carey to entice HINO of Japan to build a factory in his state. Considering the limited size of the market for buses, it is interesting that MAN is engaged in building a facility in North Carolina and Neoplan in Lamar, Colorado. There are those who think that this is not only a means of satisfying the 51 percent "Buy American," but of readying for a possible later move into the far more profitable and larger market for heavy trucks—just as the Japanese have already invaded the light "pick-up" market.

Outlook

Just as the foreign automobile manufacturers have entered the American market and several have built or are contemplating building plants, so it is with the mass transportation market. Foreign transit vehicle firms are capturing markets and some are building facilities here. In addition to the MAN and Neoplan plants, Bombardier of Canada is building a plant in Barre, Vermont for the manufacture of locomotive-drawn rail passenger cars. Foreign suppliers like Kawasaki and Breda for the present have arranged for assembling their transit cars in plants of American companies that were formerly prime bidders themselves.

Obviously, as in the case of the automobile industry, American preeminence has already faded. Foreign competition is taking a major share of the American market. The saga of opportunity lost through bureaucratic bungling on the part of government, of underestimation of the tasks of design and production by industry and of the unrealistic expectations of some of the transit operators is sad to recount.

Possible Remedies

The cures for these sad conditions correspond to their causes. American manufacturers, or would-be manufacturers, must improve their understanding of the new technologies in their specific application to the harsh realities of urban mass transit. Any new generation of vehicle must be tested both in prototype and in first production runs in the actualities of service conditions. A realistic estimation of production time, costs, weights and guarantees is a prerequisite for successful bidding. After all, it was the domestic manufacturers' defaults that really opened the door to foreign competition.

Transit operators, and those who control them, need to recognize that novelty and difference for their own sake can be counter-productive. The failures of the automated BART system and its expensive retrofit toward the more conventional were chastening experiences. It should be recognized that there is an economic and operating advantage in requiring service-proven equipment, commonality of components and a systems-engineering capability that ensures component synergy.

Together with the governments that control them, the transit operators should reexamine the competitive bidding requirements that require contracts go to the lowest bidder. Transit operators ought to be given more latitude in the pre-qualification of bidders and greater freedom to select the proven producer and product as against unknown quantities. The initial cost of the transit vehicle should not be the only consideration. Procurement should take into account maintainability, repair prospects, availability of spare parts and skilled labor to service the equipment. Laying out a realistic program for vehicle purchase over a time period, and fixing specifications for a succession of orders in that time frame would benefit both the operator and the supplier.

Reduce Government Involvement

Significant governmental changes are indicated if we are to eliminate the layers of approvals and bureaucratic second guessing that now burdens transit authorities' decisions. The multiple reviews by local, state and federal government agencies, and the controls by compliance agencies of various sorts plus comptrollers and auditors—not to mention legal officers—have done more to retard than advance transit.

Similarly, government mandates for detailed specifications have failed to build a better bus. Costly requirements like a wheelchair lift for all transit buses are in fact hamstringing transit progress and should be reconsidered and eliminated.

There must also be more consistency and continuity of governmental policy and administration. From 1965 to date, the Federal Mass Transit Program has had 15 different administrators. Only two of them had actually previously administered transit systems. The "on-the-job training" of UMTA administrators stands in stark contrast to the continuity of policy and direction of the Federal Highway Administration. By the same token, the research and development activities of the federal government ought to give greater emphasis to applied technology that can bring more immediate assistance to urban transit. To be sure, it is interesting to espouse and finance studies of "PRT" (personal rapid transit)—individual pods carrying one or a few people moving over guideways at high speeds with three-second intervals between them. Nonetheless, such projects are a far cry from today's and tomorrow's mass transit problems—not to mention their energy implications.

The "Transit Renaissance" will continue. Economic, energy and environmental imperatives dictate it. America's urban transportation systems will be modernized and expanded. There is really no alternative. And all of this can surely entail business and jobs for American enterprise. Realization of these possibilities absolutely necessitates, however, a "new awakening" on the part of the relevant echelons of American management and labor.

The "Transit Renaissance" can still be followed by a "Transit Industry Reformation"!

RUMBLING TOWARD RUIN[5]

Nearly 30 million people ride subways, buses, trolleys or commuter trains every weekday in the U.S. Yet everywhere mass transit is either stalling or rumbling inexorably toward ruin. Items:

—In Philadelphia last week, a bumper-to-bumper proces-

[5] Reprint of article by Ellie McGrath, staff writer. *Time.* 117:12–15. Mr. 30, '81. Copyright 1981 Time Inc. All rights reserved. Reprinted by permission from TIME.

sion of cars, sometimes ten miles long, inched into the city while subways, buses and trolleys stood idle, sidelined by a strike of 5,000 transit workers, the fourth such in six years. Thousands of commuters from the city's outskirts tried to get downtown via Conrail, but that overtaxed railroad line had to leave hundreds stranded on platforms. Some of the 400,000 Philadelphians who rely on public transit took to bicycles to get to work. The strike, sparked by union protests over the hiring of part-time help and a decision to require maintenance workers to pass proficiency tests, is costing the city $3 million a day in business and keeping 15 percent of schoolchildren at home.

—In Birmingham, the bus system has been shut down for more than three weeks because of insufficient funding. Some 30,000 riders have been affected, and the school system has signed a contract with the Yellow Cab Co. to provide transportation until the end of the school year. The only proposed solution to the shutdown: nearly halving the 43 routes to 22 and operating only from 7 A.M. to 7 P.M., weekdays, a 65 percent cutback in daily service.

—In Chicago, the nation's second largest transit system (1 million subway, el and bus passengers a day) is going flat broke while the state legislature bickers over funding. Businesses and commuters are already reserving hotel rooms, forming car pools and making other contingency plans for a shutdown that could come as early as this week.

—Boston, which closed down its entire transit system for 26 hours last December, has just enough money to operate its subways and buses (300,000 riders) through the fall. City officials have already been forced to lay off 100 of its 6,700 transit workers, and only narrowly averted a walkout last week by postponing the layoffs of an additional 220 employees.

—In New York, whose transit system is the nation's largest (5 million daily users) and may also be its worst, already beleaguered straphangers were horrified to read headlines predicting a $1.55 fare by the summer of 1983 (*vs.* 60¢ [75¢] today and 30¢ in 1970) in return for steadily deteriorating service in graffiti-sprayed cars.

How did the U.S. transport itself into this mess? Three groups contributed mightily: pusillanimous politicians who refused to risk their constituents' wrath by asking for fare increases when they were unquestionably essential; inept managers who, despite in many cases handsome salaries and generous expense accounts, proved incapable of managing; and inflexible unions that pushed labor costs sky-high (they account for 77 percent of Chicago's operating expenses).

Aggravating the situation were a number of long-term trends. In the 1950s, transit ridership declined precipitously. Americans fell in love with the automobile, honeymooned on new highways and married into the suburbs. Subways and buses were not part of the post-World War II American dream. When the energy crisis hit in 1973, the country found that its railroad beds had deteriorated and its subways were falling apart. The Federal Government called for more efficient public transit and urged private companies to design a better bus. Mass transit was going to be the methadone that would help America withdraw from its addiction to foreign oil. It would unclog crowded highways and improve the quality of air. Besides, it was an economic necessity: people needed a reliable means of getting to work without being exhausted in the process; businesses needed a way to get customers downtown.

Public transportation is in hot demand again, but today no one wants to pick up the tab. A decade ago, to lure people back to mass transit, city and state officials made the mistake of holding fares to unrealistically low levels. From 1970 to 1975, while inflation was rising nearly 40 percent, fares were not increased at all in many cities; in some, they actually decreased. Mass transit was the closest thing to a free ride.

As labor and energy costs continued to shoot up, fares generally were paying only about half the operating costs. Increased ridership actually exacerbated the problem: rush-hour crowds require heavier overhead, but do not generate enough revenue to cover all off-hour operations. A pattern emerged in which budget deficits were picked up by the Federal Government or, more often, the states. The politics of mass transit sharpened old rivalries: downstate *vs.* upstate, rural *vs.* urban.

Like many U.S. voters, Ronald Reagan does not see urban mass transit as a high national priority. Says the President: "There is no reason for someone in Sioux Falls to pay federal taxes so that someone in Los Angeles can get to work on time by public transportation." Federal grants for major construction projects in 1981 will total $3.3 billion; operating subsidies, $1 billion. The Reagan Administration would like to limit, if not eliminate, this aid. High on the Reagan hit list is funding for any new mass transit projects (usually 80 percent federal, 20 percent state), throwing a wrench into planning in Los Angeles and Houston. Construction will proceed on projects already under way—subways in Atlanta and Baltimore, an elevated line in Miami. But some planned extensions are in jeopardy, and transit officials fear that many existing systems will be in trouble without federal help.

Such fears could prove self-fulfilling. Transportation Secretary Drew Lewis has indicated that he also favors slowly eliminating operating subsidies in order to force systems to become cost-effective. Says he: "We do not plan simply to walk away from the transit systems, because we realize that to do so would be to shut down most of them."

Although the average city gets only 13 percent of its operating budget from Washington, cutbacks are bound to mean rising transit fares, reduced services and greater demand for local and state subsidies. Such cutbacks will hurt small cities more than large ones. New York derives less than 10 percent of its operating expenses from federal subsidies, but Corpus Christi gets 69 percent, Grand Rapids 44 percent and Peoria 35 percent. Lewis contends that rehabilitating existing systems will be a top priority. Says he: "We're trying to emphasize large cities, older cities over new systems."

Nowhere does a system need rehabilitation more than New York City. Its subways are a filthy, Dantesque netherworld, plagued not merely by delays (one train in every ten is late) but by violent crime (18 murders, 12,000 muggings, robberies and other felonies in the past year). The Metropolitan Transportation Authority (MTA) carries one of every six people using public transit in the entire nation. The city cannot function without it. During a ten-day strike last spring, New York firms lost about $100 million in sales each workday.

After the 1980 strike, the MTA, already running $400 million in the red, raised the fare from 50¢ to 60¢. Even without a cutback in federal funding, the price of a token could rise to $1 by summer. One survey shows that 50 percent of New York's riders would willingly pay the dollar if it would mean safer, more efficient service. But the higher fare is unlikely to bring any such improvements. Although the massive system would cost $55 billion to replace, only $300 million a year is being spent on rehabilitation and improvement, $700 million short of what experts say is needed. The Reagan focus on capital improvements may come just in time. Although the accepted life span of a subway car is 35 years, 567 of the MTA's 8,500 cars are more than 30 years old. About a quarter of them are out of service at any given time for maintenance. Soon after shiny new cars were introduced, they had to be withdrawn when they developed cracks in their undercarriages. Admits MTA Member Steven Berger: "The only way at this point to fix things is to shut down the system for a week and call in a faith healer."

To make matters still worse, New York has been facing a congressional mandate to equip subway stations and buses for the handicapped. The MTA estimates that this would cost $1.4 billion over the next 30 years, plus $100 million a year in operating funds. The Reagan Administration may relent and allow New York to provide special but separate facilities for the handicapped.

President Reagan, however, has reaffirmed support for Manhattan's Westway, a six-lane superhighway slated to run for 4.6 miles along the Hudson River. The highway, with an estimated price tag of $1.7 billion, would receive 90 percent of its funding from the Federal Government. New York City Mayor Edward Koch has blocked the project in an effort to get parallel funds from Albany for mass transit improvements or to get Governor Hugh Carey to ask Washington to trade in highway funds for transit money.

In Boston, the finance fight is becoming another Battle of Bunker Hill. Until citizens passed the tax-cutting Proposition 2½ in November, the state legislature regularly bailed out the Massachusetts Bay Transit Authority (MBTA), which serves 79 communities. The 1981 MBTA budget was set at $6 million below the 1980 budget of $340 million, and already the system has exceeded its monthly allocations by nearly $2.4 million. At this rate, the MBTA will be broke by the fall.

Last week MBTA Director Barry Locke laid off 45 executives and 100 employees (not including 200 "door guards," who pull down as much as $33,000 a year for making sure that automatically operated doors open and close). Another 250 MBTA personnel are slated to be laid off April 3. Fares were doubled from a ridiculously low 25¢ to 50¢ last June. Locke had planned to eliminate Sunday service and school bus transportation but limited the cuts in the face of protests. Two subway stations have been shut for a saving of $294,000, and more stations are expected to be closed on weekends. But even those cuts will not be enough to keep the system solvent.

The Chicago Transit Authority (CTA) also has severe money problems. Chicago's bus drivers and motormen are the highest paid in the nation: $24,689 after 42 months. The CTA raised fares from 60¢ to 80¢ this January and promptly lost 6 percent of its riders. During the past two years the Federal Government has sent $143 million to help underwrite expenses, but such grants are bound to be cut. The projected deficit for 1981: $150 million.

Not all the crises involve antiquated subway systems. The prototype of modern transit, the San Francisco region's $1.7 billion, 71-mile Bay Area Rapid Transit (BART) has had problems as complex as its technology. Says American Public Transit Association Spokesman Al Engelken: "We were going to the moon in the '60s, and we figured we could just slap space-age technology into the subways. But what works on the moon doesn't always work in an urban environment." Indeed, BART's fully automated "train control system" was too finely tuned to withstand daily transit pressures and constantly broke down.

From the day it opened in 1972, BART never attracted enough passengers to pay its way. After a fire broke out in its high-technology San Francisco-Oakland tube beneath the bay in 1979, killing one and hospitalizing 40, ridership plummeted from 150,000 a day to 110,000. By 1979 losses were more than $6 million a year. A 1980 fare increase (from 30¢ to 50¢) sent another 8 percent of the riders scurrying elsewhere for transportation. By extending its hours from 8 P.M. to midnight, improving maintenance and getting trains to run pretty much on time, however, BART has now brought ridership up to 165,000 people.

New systems have benefited from BART's mistakes. The year-old San Francisco subway, which runs about 30 miles and costs only $333 million, shares tunnels with BART and daily transports 100,000 people without hitches. In Washington, D.C. the Metro has been a mass transit showcase. Stations with vaulted ceilings resemble underground cathedrals. Says Engelken: "It's accident-free, clean, safe and on time." But the system cost $71.3 million a mile (vs. BART's $22.5 million), and all of it was built at federal expense.

So far, 37 of Metro's planned 101 miles are finished, with work progressing rapidly on lines linking affluent Maryland and Virginia suburbs to downtown. Nearly 300,000 people ride it every day. But the graduated fare, ranging from 50¢ to $2.05, would have to be more than doubled to make the system pay for itself. Losses for 1981 are estimated to be $131.5 million. While the Reagan Administration has promised at least another 40 miles of Metro, the routes that would run through Washington's poorer black neighborhoods remain a low priority.

The Metro may turn out to be the Rolls-Royce of American mass transit. Because of its high cost, transit planners question whether many cities have a dense enough population to deserve "heavy rail" or underground transit. The Department of Transportation rejected Houston's request for a

$1 billion heavy rail line last year. Detroit too is in limbo over a proposed 15-mile light railway system linking the city with its northern suburbs. Miami still gets funding for its $867 million, 21-mile elevated rail line, but its downtown "people mover" may fall victim to federal budget cuts.

The country's newest subway system, Atlanta's MARTA, opened its first twelve-mile segment in 1979 and is scheduled to operate a second segment from downtown to the new airport in 1985. The availability of federal funding will determine how much more of the $3 billion rapid-rail system gets built. In Baltimore, construction is half completed on an eight-mile rail line from downtown to the northwest suburbs, but the second leg, in an area where a 15-mile auto commute can take an hour is in jeopardy. The projected cost of the undertaking: $958 million.

Even Los Angeles, land of the ubiquitous auto, has made what is proving to be an ill-timed move toward mass transit. With buses now moving 1.25 million riders a day, voters approved a .5 percent increase in the 6 percent sales tax last November to finance a metro rail system. One arm would have linked downtown Los Angeles' Union Station with North Hollywood and the San Fernando Valley, an 18-mile project costing $2 billion. Other plans called for a 2.9-mile downtown monorail "people mover" and two elevated systems along the Santa Ana Freeway corridor (17 miles) and the Harbor Freeway corridor (20 miles). With federal money drying up and Proposition 13 in effect, there is now little hope that such projects will be built.

One city in California is making do without federal funds by looking to the past. San Diego will resurrect its reliable old fixed-rail trolley system this summer. Using an existing railroad right-of-way, the city has upgraded the roadbed and laid new rails for a 16-mile run between downtown San Diego and the Mexican border. The cost: $5 million a mile, 7 percent of what the Washington Metro cost and 1.3 percent of what New York's Westway would cost. Featuring a $1 fare, the bright red "Tijuana Trolley" is expected to carry about 300,-000 passengers a day. The funding comes from state gas taxes and the cars come from Germany.

Of course, trolley lines—even good ones—are hardly the answer to the nation's transit woes. And it is beyond dispute that, despite America's romance with the automobile, major U.S. cities—like major cities anywhere in the industrialized world—must have effective mass transit systems if they are to survive. The economics of OPEC and the hazards of air pollution leave no other choice. The question is not whether something should be done to make such systems work. The question is what should be done, and how urgently.

SICK AND INGLORIOUS TRANSIT[6]

Irate New Yorkers are pushing past the token booths and ducking under the turnstiles. In Philadelphia, commuter trains are plastered with white cardboard notices announcing the end of service on Aug. 30. In Chicago, suburbanites are so infuriated by fare increases that they are threatening to desert their leafy outposts. "I'm going to move into the city," vows Bob Madden, 24, a printing company salesman who lives 24 miles from downtown in Deerfield, Ill. "I could probably afford to commute, but I've got better things to do with my money."

In a clutch of the nation's largest cities, mass-transit systems—already rumbling toward hell—have never seemed closer to that infernal destination. Plagued by crumbling equipment, dismal service and deepening deficits, several cities boosted fares this month just to keep their systems sputtering along. As a further sign that there may be no light at the end of the mass-transit tunnel, the Administration promises to phase out by 1985 federal operating subsidies for bus and rail systems, now running at $1.1 billion a year and making up 13 percent of total costs.

No system seems closer to stopping dead in its tracks than New York City's, the largest in the nation with 5 million daily passengers. With an operating deficit of $500 million for this

[6] Reprint of article by James Kelly, staff writer. *Time*. 118:25. Jl. 20, '81. Copyright 1981 Time Inc. All rights reserved. Reprinted by permission from TIME.

fiscal year, the state's Metropolitan Transportation Authority (MTA) two weeks ago upped subway and bus fares from 60¢ to 75¢ and raised the prices of commuter tickets on Conrail and the Long Island Railroad by an average of 25 percent. The MTA also threatened to hike fares to $1 by mid-July unless the state legislature covered an estimated shortfall of $331 million. The legislature finally approved a Band-Aid package of new taxes last week, including a .75 percent tax on the gross receipts of oil companies, that will raise $800 million over the next two years. But MTA Chairman Richard Ravitch is making no promises that fares will not go up again before 1983. "I can't guarantee anything," he shrugs.

At the same time, the New York Transit Authority is proposing to cut back its maintenance program and curtail service. The city's subways are already a Stygian underworld, with filthy, overcrowded trains careening at high speeds one moment, then stalling for eternities with lights out and passengers steaming. "When I first rode the subways, I thought I was on a prison train," says Sashi Ray, who emigrated from India in 1976. "Now, when I compare the streets of Calcutta to the subways, I must confess the subways are by far the worse."

In Philadelphia, the Southeastern Pennsylvania Transportation Authority (SEPTA) raised fares on the city's bus, trolley and subway lines from 65¢ to 70¢ last week—the third hike since 1978, when a ride cost 45¢. If that were not bad enough, Conrail is threatening to shut down its commuter lines around Philadelphia, which carry 65,000 people on weekdays, unless SEPTA increases its annual subsidy from $93 million to $99 million. SEPTA Chairman David Girard-di-Carlo insists that his agency is broke and may seek a court order to keep Conrail behind the throttle. If he fails, SEPTA may have to run the trains. Complains Girard-diCarlo: "We can't rush into operating a $100 million operation overnight."

In Boston, the Massachusetts Bay Transportation Authority (MBTA) is considering upping bus fares from 25¢ to 50¢ and subway tokens from 50¢ to 75¢ on Aug. 1. Since most riders take both bus and subway on their way to work, the average round trip will cost $2.50. Admits Phil Shapiro, staff director of the MBTA's advisory board: "These hikes may end up not being competitive with the automobile." The MBTA appears to have no choice: the agency will exhaust its annual budget of $337 million by Thanksgiving.

In Chicago, fares on the city's buses and subways rose by a dime to 90¢ last week, a 50 percent boost over last December and now the highest in the nation. Transfers cost an extra 10¢, and most riders end up paying $2 for a round trip. The region's 140,000 suburban commuters must dig even more deeply into their wallets: the Regional Transportation Authority (RTA) raised its fares last week by an average 57 percent. Chicago Attorney Laurie Shatsoff last December bought a condominium in Vernon Hills, about 40 miles outside the city, and since then she has watched the cost of her monthly train pass rocket from $59 to $141.95. "It's now like my mortgage," she protests. "I'm just glad my secretary lives in the city. Otherwise, I couldn't afford to pay her."

The Chicago fare hikes are in part the result of sniping between the state legislature and Chicago Mayor Jane Byrne; when Springfield offered the Chicago Transit Authority $425 million over the next three years, Byrne huffed that an additional $45 million was needed, and the entire aid package collapsed. The city's fare hike even poses its own mechanical problem: the dollar bills deposited by bus riders jam the fare boxes. To combat the problem, CTA officials instructed its ticket takers to hand out Susan B. Anthony dollars as change, but passengers are refusing to accept the unpopular coin. "I don't give them out, people complain too much," says one cashier.

In Atlanta, fares rose from 50¢ to 60¢ on July 1, and may jump again if the Metropolitan Atlanta Rapid Transit Authority (MARTA) has to pay its bus drivers an additional cost of living allowance. In Houston, maintenance men ripped out the sealed windows of a covey of new $86,000 buses last year when the air conditioning broke down, and riders this sum-

mer are cooled by the occasional breeze—and drenched by
the occasional rainstorm.

Once among the finest in the industrialized world, the nation's urban mass-transit systems obviously are no longer
bound for glory. Riders, already deserting subways and buses
in many cities, may start leaving in droves. Says Costas
Servas, a frustrated passenger on New York's Seventh Avenue
line: "The people have had enough."

NO-FARE TRANSIT—A VALUABLE EXPERIMENT[7]

Americans cannot continue indefinitely their current consumption of petroleum-produced goods and services. Already, the American family is spending close to 20 percent of
its income on transportation costs, mostly for gasoline for private automobiles. That cost will rise even more—quite a bit
more—by 1981.

Hand-in-hand with this consumption of energy comes
pollution. And the high cost of transportation is depriving the
less advantaged of necessary mobility. One of the ways to
combat these urgent problems is mass transit and a concept
receiving increased attention in terms of energy use, pollution abatement and reviving cities is no-fare transit, a program that recognizes urban mass transit as an essential public
service, much like police and fire services.

The program is designed to attract motorists out of their
cars and onto mass transit for their daily commute to and
from work, and to provide transportation service and mobility for all groups of citizens.

The Amalgamated Transit Union, which has been promoting the concept for more than a decade, has recently
added the concept of low-fare transit to its proposals, with
low-fare defined as a cost not to exceed 25 cents for a system-

[7] Reprint of article by Joe Brady, director of publications, Amalgamated Transit
Union. *AFL-CIO American Federationist.* Je. '80 (special issue of the official monthly magazine of the AFL-CIO).

wide ride. All studies indicate that low-fare programs would produce nearly the same results as no-fare programs. At the same time, a low-fare program would answer some of the no-fare critics' charges about revenue losses and joyriding. So whenever no-fare is mentioned in general terms, low-fare is also inferred.

No-fare transit was first proposed at least as early as 1922 in Boston, but it wasn't until the energy crisis took hold in the mid-1970s that it began to get deserved attention. Even now, with the continuing effects of that energy crisis, especially the exorbitant gasoline prices, no-fare transit is far from a reality. But progress is being made.

Early in 1979, two communities—Denver and Mercer County, N.J., which is the Trenton area—completed year-long experiments in non-rush hour no-fare demonstration projects funded by the Urban Mass Transportation Administration (UMTA) of the U.S. Department of Transportation. Preliminary reports on both experiments offer some interesting insights.

Denver witnessed a daily ridership increase of 53,000 passengers, 19,000 of whom said they would have made their trip by auto if it were not for the no-fare program. Trenton saw a weekly ridership increase of 16,000 to a total of 150,000, with some 7,500 saying they would have used their auto under normal conditions.

These experiments were the first sustained, documented studies of no-fare transit and its effects on communities, but other transit systems throughout the country have or are staging similar programs.

—Seattle initiated a no-fare program in its downtown business district in 1973. It soon produced a 56 percent increase in ridership and three-fold increase in service. The program has been expanded and is still in operation today.

—Portland, Ore., established its version of no-fare transit in its business district in January 1975. Called "Fareless Square," the program almost immediately produced a nine-fold increase in transit ridership.

—Dallas introduced a no-fare system similar to Seattle's

and Portland's in 1975 and within three months daily ridership nearly tripled.

—Knoxville instituted such a program in 1977 and within
a year monthly ridership had more than doubled.

—Albany, N.Y., began a similar operation in late 1978 and
within a few weeks ridership had more than doubled.

—Pittsburgh, Honolulu, Nashville, Syracuse, N.Y., Commerce, Calif., and countless other major cities and small communities are trying no-fare/low-fare programs and achieving
similar results.

When no-fare transit eliminates the fares on transit systems, it is made possible generally by levying a tax—gasoline,
income or whatever—on all potential transit users and beneficiaries within a geographical area to operate the transit system. Other methods of financing have been used, but the tax
is the most accepted method. In effect, these taxes are a pre-
payment for transit service and facilities offered by the city.
In return, the entire population is entitled to access to public
transportation at any time for any purpose.

For years the transit industry had been in decay with annual passenger fares dropping from 19 billion in 1945 to 5.5
billion in 1973. During this time industry's answer to decreased ridership and to corresponding decreased revenues
was always the same: increased fares. It has been proven time
and again that each 1 percent increase in fares produced a 0.2
to 0.33 decrease in ridership, which would start the vicious
circle all over again—further increases in fares, further decreases in riders. In trying to keep their financial heads above
water, the operators were drowning the transit systems.

In 1945, when 19 billion fare-paying passengers boarded
the nation's transit network, the average fare was about 7
cents; in 1973 when only 5.5 billion paying passengers uti-
lized the transit systems, the average fare was approximately
32 cents. Meanwhile employment in the transit industry
dropped from 242,000 in 1945 to 139,000 in 1972.

The energy crisis of late 1973 and early 1974 provoked the
first reversal in this decline.

The crisis focused the spotlight on America's love affair

with the automobile. Eighty percent of all American families own at least one car—an increase of more than 40 percent over the last 15 years. The number of two-car families has risen over 400 percent in the past 10 years. The American Automobile Association estimates that car drivers logged more than 900 billion miles in 1973—an increase of 51 percent in the past 10 years.

There are approximately 51 million Americans who daily commute to and from work by car.

When the 1973-74 energy crunch brought long gas lines and an awakening awareness of America's complete dependence on the gas-hungry automobile, mass transit ridership increased 6 percent overall in 1974—paying and non-paying customers—for a total of 7 billion passengers.

But the industry was ill-prepared for such an influx of new riders. Although it did manage to cope with the situation, it could have done much more. The industry probably recorded the passenger increases not so much because of what it did, but simply because it was there at a time when car owners found gasoline hard to get and quite expensive when it could be obtained. Furthermore, the knowledge that the entire country literally could be shut down in a matter of months simply by turning off the gas pumps probably "frightened" many people onto mass transit.

Since then, mass transit ridership has continued to increase until the current time, when more than 8 billion passengers are riding annually.

The energy crisis was not a challenge to the transit industry; if anything, it was a windfall blessing. The industry's true challenge lies in the immediate future. The gas is flowing again and even though the price averages a dollar a gallon more than pre-crisis levels, motorists are paying the bill as long as they get the gas.

It is anybody's guess what the future holds. But one thing is virtually certain: gasoline, no matter what its availability, is going to cost even more. Which means the urban transit industry has within its reach an opportunity and responsibility not only to hold the riders it gained during the energy crisis and since, but also to add even greater numbers as motorists search for alternative means of transportation.

But the industry must be prepared—or better, anticipatory. It can stand pat and confirm many peoples' suspicions that mass transit consists of high fares, dilapidated vehicles, overcrowded rush-hour conditions and inflexible routes and schedules. Or it can initiate programs to put all these suspicions to rest and to make urban mass transit an attractive, alternative means of transportation.

Obviously, one such program is no-fare or prepaid transit. The elimination of the fare box, in conjunction with other incentives and certain restraints, can rejuvenate urban mass transit, while at the same time ease the demands for energy, alleviate the pollution problems and once again make the inner city a viable area.

Besides the energy and environmental aspects there is another factor which tends to make no-fare transit a more acceptable program. For years, transit systems throughout the country were under the control of private operators whose sole concern was profits. However, from 1968 to now there has been a sharp trend from private to public ownership, until today more than 95 percent of the major transit systems are publicly owned and operated.

The implications of public ownership are essentially threefold: a transit system is no longer required to turn a profit; it need not be self-sustaining; and it should provide the best possible service as determined by the public interest.

Public takeovers also have resulted in the improvement of urban mass transit. From 1964 to 1974, some $3.2 billion in capital assistance grants to improve urban transit systems was made available by the federal government. In addition, transit systems also can receive assistance for operating expenditures. These funds, it should be remembered, are taxpayers' monies.

This trend to public ownership accompanied by federal financial assistance and the possibility to cut down on energy consumption, pollution and congestion by attracting the car driver onto mass transit, coupled with the industry's dismal record at maintaining a viable service through fare increases, makes the case for no-fare transit even more appealing.

Further support for such a program is contained in a 1975 study entitled "Energy, the Economy and Mass Transit," sponsored by the Office of Technology Assessment of the U.S. Congress.

Undertaken to examine the interrelationships between federal urban mass transit policy and programs and changes in the level of national energy supplies and the condition of the economy, the study concluded that initiation of a no-fare transit program would result in an estimated 40 to 60 percent increase in transit ridership. In addition, it concluded that the improvement of system service to patrons by eliminating the time and inconvenience of collecting fares could result in an additional 10 to 15 percent increase in ridership.

According to the study, "no-fare transit would produce the largest increase in transit ridership of any action that has been considered." It went on to say that additional advantages of no-fare would include:

—Greater increases in off-peak ridership and therefore better utilization of manpower and equipment. This would be particularly true of an off-peak no-fare program.

—Compared to most of the other actions considered, it could be implemented relatively easily on a national basis through congressional action.

—Benefits would generally be greatest among those most in need of increased mobility—the young, the elderly, the poor and many of the handicapped. No-fare during off-peak riding hours would concentrate the benefits among these groups to an even greater extent.

—It would necessarily result in an improvement of service, in part because it would do away with the inconvenience to users of having to have exact change, and in part because it would permit faster transit operation.

—The increase in ridership resulting from no-fare in peak periods would require a 40 to 70 percent increase in transit operations, thereby causing substantial increases in frequency and coverage of transit service—in itself one of the most effective actions which can be pursued. On the other hand, an off-peak no-fare program could be implemented without any peak hour increases in frequency of service, but would require substantial off-peak increases.

—No other action could produce such large-scale results so quickly. Capital investment in rapid transit systems in the same order of magnitude of $5 billion per year could probably produce similar ridership increases, but probably not within 10 to 15 years.

Before reaching these general conclusions concerning no-fare transit, the congressional study developed three packages of transit-related actions which, in certain combination, showed even more positive results accruing from no-fare transit. The three packages were: a maximum transit incentive package; a maximum auto restraint package; and a combination package incorporating maximum transit incentives and auto restraints.

Components of the maximum transit incentive package included no-fare transit; doubling the transit vehicle fleet by 1980; and no significant auto restraints (the price of gasoline was assumed to stay constant in real dollar terms).

The maximum auto restraint package included a 50 percent increase in the price of gasoline in real dollar terms; a $1.50 per day increase in the cost of commuter parking in employment areas well served by transit; and no significant transit incentive actions (the transit fleet would increase in size only as necessary to cover 90 percent of the increase in peak period ridership).

The combination package included no-fare transit; doubling the transit vehicle fleet by 1980; a 50 percent increase in the real price of gasoline; and a $1.50 per day increase in the cost of commuter parking in employment areas well served by transit.

In each of these packages the study assumed there would be no limitation on the availability of gasoline. The effects of limitations on the supply of crude oil were also considered. It assumed three alternative energy decreases:

—Mild—decrease of 1 million barrels of crude oil per day by 1976 followed by a 3 percent per year growth in consumption.

—Moderate—decrease of 3 million barrels of crude oil per day by 1977 followed by a 1.5 percent per year growth rate;

—Severe—a decrease of 6 million barrels of crude per day by 1980.

The study also took into account probable economic conditions during the next year and their effect on the different packages.

Taken alone, the transit incentive package would be limited in its potential to promote large reductions in the consumption of transportation energy because less than 50 percent of the new riders attracted by major actions of this type would otherwise have been auto drivers, according to the study.

Taken alone, auto restraint actions tend to concentrate associated transit ridership increases in the peak period, leading to more than proportional increases in manpower and capital requirements, according to the study.

However, the study concludes that by initiating the combination package of transit incentives and auto restraints the gains in ridership would be tremendous, and the potential exists for using the gas and parking tax revenues to cover transit deficits.

The study states, "The maximum transit incentive package and combined package have very similar impacts on the transit industry. Costs, deficits, manpower and rolling stock requirements are identical in both packages. The only differences are that the combined package has higher ridership and also has the potential for use of gas and parking tax revenues to cover transit deficits.

"Both packages assume a doubling of transit service and

the elimination of fares. These assumptions double the operating costs and eliminate fare box revenue, thus making the entire cost of operations equal to the deficit. In 1974, the national transit operating expenses were just over $3 billion. In 1974, a doubling of operations while eliminating fares would have created a $6 billion deficit, compared to the $1.3 billion deficit in 1974 when fares were collected.

"Deficits of these proportions would justify increases in funding for research and development of techniques and systems with lower operating costs. In addition, very large increases in ridership of 100 to 120 percent would accompany this package.

"The combined package incorporates the two revenue producing actions used in the auto restraint package . . . these restraints could produce about $13 billion annually, more than enough to cover the transit deficit.

"The doubling of transit service will require a doubling of the transit labor force or an addition of about 150,000 employees. With the addition of the employment multiplier in service-related industries, the total employment impact of this expansion of transit service is an increase of about 225,-000 jobs.

"The additional rolling stock required will equal 3,000 new rail cars . . . and 50,000 new buses by 1980. Orders for these additional vehicles will strain the capacity of the rail and bus manufacturers. However, with an increase in bus plant capacity and significantly greater production in the latter years, these vehicles could be produced and in operation by 1980.

"The cost of these new vehicles would total $4.75 billion and would require about 390,000 man-years to produce them. Since this production would be spread over six years, the average additional annual employment generated by these increases in transit's rolling stock would be about 65,000 jobs for the six years of production."

The study concludes that the combined package would have produced ridership increases of 100 to 120 percent, conserved energy by maintaining efficient passenger miles-per-vehicle consumption, would have more than financed itself through the gas and parking tax, and would have generated in the neighborhood of 500,000 jobs in the transit industry and related industries by . . . 1980.

The highly favorable results through the initiation of a no-fare transit program or combination transit incentive/auto restraint program envisioned in this study necessarily assume the establishment of some complimentary factors, such as priority bus lanes, park and ride facilities, dial-a-bus service, efficient feeder lines, priority traffic signal controls for transit, exclusive bus lanes, transit shelters and stations, a position reorientation of the federal highway program to accommodate transit rather than the automobile, and a federal policy affecting land development more closely tied to the provision of public transportation services.

All in all, no-fare transit comes across as a far more effective replacement for the private automobile than any other alternative now under consideration. In terms of immediate availability, lesser cost and greater potential for making all U.S. citizens more mobile, no-fare transit is a far better answer to the problems of our cities.

One of the main objections raised is that no-fare transit would lead to an abuse of the system. In answer it should be noted that adults are not known to ride inner city transit systems simply for the enjoyment of riding, they are generally headed for a specific destination. There might, indeed, be some initial abuse by joyriding children, but children generally tire of such foolishness after a short while. If necessary, local regulations can be instituted to deal with problem cases.

In fact, a report prepared by UMTA on the no-fare experiments in Denver and Mercer County, states that youth joyriding and rowdyism were problems. However, it goes on to say: "At each site, local newspapers made much of the issue, perhaps amplifying its magnitude in the eyes of the public. With the advent of summer, attention to the issue and the number of reported incidents declined at both sites. Whether or not there was overreaction to the initial effect, the problems seem to have been largely transitory."

Another objection is that the solution to mass transit problems is improved service rather than reduction or elimination of fares. Improved service is to be applauded, but it has historically been accompanied by increased fares and, as has been pointed out, fare hikes are the sure road to bankruptcy. Fare hikes mean more and more cars on our city streets, which is exactly what the country does not need.

An oft-heard argument is that by attracting more riders through fare elimination and improved services, transit systems will become too crowded. This is exactly why provisions are made in any discussion of no-fare transit for increasing the size of transit fleets.

Still others claim that no-fare transit "is just another freebie," similar to welfare aid. Obviously, the financing mechanisms mentioned here and in any discussion of the issue negate that argument. And it is interesting to note that you rarely hear these same people decrying the billions spent annually on subsidizing highway construction to facilitate the automobile.

This is not to say that initiation of a no-fare program would be the panacea for all transportation problems, or that it would be without any problems. Like any new undertaking it most likely would have wrinkles and bugs that would have to be corrected. But viewed in the context of the current situation of mass transit in this country and the overwhelming benefit of reduced automobile usage, any problems connected with initiation of the no-fare program would be miniscule in comparison.

Since World War II this nation has become a land of "suburban sprawl." With increased mobility afforded by the automobile, people began to move farther and farther from the inner city, indiscriminately erecting homes and communities. No longer were traditional avenues of transportation adhered to. The land became crisscrossed with miles and miles of concrete ribbon created for the convenience of the automobile. Federal land policies, coupled with federal highway projects, encouraged this flight to the suburbs, and the inner cities were allowed to deteriorate, existing mainly as the work center for the suburban dwellers. Traffic jams became the order of the day as 51 million people swarmed into the cities to work. And as the cities crumbled, business and industry began shifting to the suburbs, creating unbelievable traffic flows into and out of the cities. Those confined to the city—generally the minorities, the elderly, the handicapped, the poor—were left dependent on mass transportation for mobility, and the transit systems dependent on the poor, the handicapped, the elderly for survival.

There are numerous factors which must be weighed when contemplating implementation of a no-fare transit system. Is the cost and effort necessary for such implementation worth it to free the moribund city dwellers, to give them mobility so they can get to where the jobs are, to get to the supermarkets? Is it worth it to ease racial polarization and tensions? Is it worth it when it can help restore an environment that currently is seen only through a haze of polluting smog? Is it worth it when it could help free valuable land space for the development of recreational areas, low-income housing, cultural centers and other people-oriented projects? It is worth it when it can help cut drastically the number of people killed or maimed annually on the nation's roads.

When all the factors are weighed, the benefits of no-fare transit tip the scale heavily in its favor. This essentially is what organized labor in the United States has been saying since 1969 when it first endorsed no-fare transit.

Nothing in the intervening time has changed the union position, except it now feels that no-fare—or at least low-fare—transit is needed more urgently than ever.

If this country is serious about conserving energy, if it is serious about revitalizing its inner cities, if it is serious about cleaning up the environment, if it is serious about granting equal opportunities to all citizens, then it should look to an efficient, attractive mass transit system to help it achieve these goals.

And the best known way to provide such a transit system is through a no-fare and/or low-fare program.

IV. TAKING CARE OF THE HANDICAPPED

EDITOR'S INTRODUCTION

The term "transportation disadvantaged" began appearing in some government reports and studies only a few years ago. It refers to segments of the population unable to utilize adequate transportation modes because of low income, age or physical disability. The plight of these people is now attracting much-deserved national attention. This section surveys some transportation problems confronting the handicapped and governmental solutions.

Recent national legislation, partly resulting from citizen lobbying, has widened transportation accessibility for many handicapped Americans. Section 504 of the Rehabilitation Act of 1973, prohibits discrimination against the physically handicapped in any government-subsidized program, and has helped create barrier-free mass transit in many cities. While the article, "Equal Access—It Seemed Like A Good Idea," reprinted from *U.S. News & World Report,* describes this legislation as well-intentioned, it claims that it has been less than successful: too costly for cities and underutilized by disabled Americans. *The Congressional Quarterly Report* surveys the history of the law and analyzes its economic and political impact, suggesting that a van system might better serve the handicapped than implementation of Section 504.

EQUAL ACCESS—IT SEEMED LIKE A GOOD IDEA[1]

Washington is taking a long, second look at an obscure law that would cost bus and subway systems billions of dollars to obey—yet benefit only a relative handful of people.

[1] Reprint of article by Jeannye Thornton, associate editor. *U.S. News & World Report.* 91:45. Jl. 20, '81. Copyright 1981, U.S. News & World Report, Inc.

That law is Section 504 of the Rehabilitation Act of 1973, which requires that federally aided activities must be accessible to the handicapped.

Simple and just as that provision may seem, it has thrown the transit industry into turmoil. Bus and subway systems, many of them almost penniless, are being required to buy buses with expensive wheelchair lifts, to put elevators in all new and many existing subway and commuter-rail stations and to bear the operating costs of the new hardware.

All these expenses come as President Reagan seeks to phase out federal operating subsidies for mass transit, thereby intensifying the financial squeeze.

Worse yet, transit operators who have bought buses with wheelchair lifts and installed subway elevators report that almost no handicapped people use them. Of the 7,595 elevator riders at the 41 Washington, D.C., subway stations one day last April, the transit system reported, only 160 were in wheelchairs, blind or on crutches; the rest were able-bodied. Detroit's buses carry an average of only four wheelchair patrons a day, and those in the Los Angeles area just five.

Hunt for Alternatives

"It's idiocy to try to make whole systems—some of them old—accessible to the handicapped," remarks Alan Kiepper, general manager of the Metropolitan Atlanta Rapid Transit Authority. "We have a commitment to serve the elderly and handicapped, but it can be done in a way that doesn't slow down service and result in higher cost in acquisition and maintenance."

The message seems to have been heard. The Reagan administration is asking Congress to allow local transit operators to choose the best means of obeying the law. Two alternatives might be door-to-door van service or subsidized taxicab rides.

On another front, the U.S. Circuit Court of Appeals in Washington ruled recently that the Department of Transportation went beyond its bounds in demanding the lift buses and subway elevators. DOT is preparing temporary regulations that would allow each transit authority to serve the handicapped as it sees fit, pending further action by Congress.

When the law was enacted in 1973, few people foresaw the problems that would ensue. Section 504 was neither debated nor scarcely remarked upon in either house of Congress. Its vague wording merely said that handicapped persons cannot be denied the benefits of federal programs solely because of their handicaps, and it instructed the bureaucracy to issue necessary rules.

The former Department of Health, Education and Welfare in January, 1979, set guidelines for the other federal agencies that would have to write the actual regulations, and it told them to interpret Section 504 broadly.

"The policy option was imposed on us by the HEW guidelines," says Michael Martinez, a Transportation Department lawyer. "The concept was for 'mainline' accessibility to wheelchair users."

So DOT's regulations, when they became final in July, 1979, required that every bus and every subway, commuter and Amtrak train in the U.S. be equipped to handle people in wheelchairs. For buses, this meant that each new or renovated vehicle bought with federal help needed a wheelchair lift—at an added cost of $15,000 to $20,000 per bus.

That was only the beginning of the problems, say transit officials. Such buses have less capacity than the regular commuter buses they replace, tend to break down more frequently because of their complicated mechanisms and are delayed for 5 minutes or so each time a wheelchair user seeks to board.

"On a good day," says Conrad Mallett, director of the Detroit Transportation Department, "20 percent of the lift-equipped buses aren't working. On a bad day, it's 40 percent."

Equally stringent rules applied to subways. Each newly built station would need elevators, and each newly purchased subway car would need entrances and interior space wide enough for wheelchair users. Existing subway systems were given 30 years to meet the standards.

The cost of obeying these regulations, said the Congressional Budget Office, would be 6.8 billion dollars over the next 30 years. New York City alone faced 1.5 billion in capital costs, plus another 400 million annually in added operating expenses. New York's Metropolitan Transportation Authority decided it would be cheaper to give up all federal aid, and refused to draw up a required compliance plan.

Back to the Mat

Now, with the original rules in disrepute, the government is again forced to wrestle with a difficult, emotional question: How can the transportation needs of the handicapped best be met, and at what cost?

"It's a civil right," argues Reese Robrahn, executive director of the American Coalition of Citizens With Disabilities. "The handicapped deserve equal access. We don't think the cost issue has anything to do with civil rights. Besides, benefits would far outweigh the costs because equal access allows the handicapped to be independent."

The Reagan administration, which wants Congress to permit less costly means of obeying the 1973 law, is taking a different approach.

"Local communities are in a better position to determine what's best for them," says Arthur E. Teele, Jr., head of DOT's Urban Mass Transportation Administration. "We should be here to support their decisions. Local option allows the flexibility consistent with this approach."

EQUALITY FOR HANDICAPPED: CAN THE NATION AFFORD IT?[2]

The nation's commitment to equality and mobility for the handicapped is running up against the biggest barrier of all—money.

[2] Reprint of article by Harrison Donnelly, staff writer. *Congressional Quarterly Report.* 38:1506–9. My. 31, '80. Reprinted with permission.

Seven years after passage of the historic law, known as Section 504, that outlawed discrimination against the handicapped in federally supported programs, many people are wondering whether society can afford its full implementation—at least as it has been interpreted by the federal government so far. . . .

Section 504

For a law that was to lead to revolutionary changes in the lives of millons of people, Section 504 received amazingly little attention or debate when it was passed by Congress in 1973. One of the problems in the subsequent struggle over its interpretation has been that there was almost no legislative history to show what Congress had in mind.

Actually, the law of which Section 504 was a part, the Rehabilitation Act of 1973, was the object of an intense legislative-executive fight. President Nixon successfully vetoed the bill twice before finally signing a third version. But his objections were to the amount of money in the bill, not to Section 504.

Offered as a House floor amendment by Charles A. Vanik (D-Ohio), Section 504 was adopted by voice vote. Vanik later was quoted as saying he had no idea of the potential cost effects of the amendment.

Section 504 states: "No otherwise qualified handicapped individual in the United States . . . shall, solely by reason of his handicap, be excluded from participation in, be denied benefits of, or be subjected to discrimination under any program or activity receiving federal financial assistance."

Putting that blanket injunction into practice, by writing specific federal regulations, proved to be a difficult and time-consuming task. It was not until 1976 that President Ford ordered the Department of Health, Education and Welfare (HEW) to provide guidance to other federal agencies in meeting the law's mandate.

But HEW officials under Ford, citing the lack of congressional direction, were reluctant to act. When the Carter administration came into office and the regulations still did not come out, leading handicapped groups occupied HEW offices, demanding that they be issued.

HEW finally issued regulations for its own activities in April 1977, and for other departments in January 1978. Other federal agencies have also had to issue their own Section 504 regulations. While they generally have not been as controversial as in transportation and higher education, they have had a major impact on areas such as health care, housing and elementary and secondary education.

Transportation

While Section 504 extends to all activities of the federal government, it is in the area of federally subsidized mass transit that the conflict over handicapped rights is the sharpest. The cost of making public transportation available to the handicapped has become an increasingly important issue as inflation and energy shortages put additional pressures on transit systems.

Mass transit has also been the object of the most successful counterattack by critics of the Carter administration's interpretation of the requirements of Section 504. Lobbying by the American Public Transit Association (APTA) has helped to win House committee approval of an amendment that would allow local transit systems to decide for themselves how best to serve the handicapped.

The APTA turned to Congress for help after a federal court ruled in February against its lawsuit charging that the Department of Transportation's (DOT) regulations went beyond what Congress had in mind when it passed Section 504.

Whatever the philosophical differences over handicapped rights, the controversy over transit accessibility is essentially one of allocation of a limited amount of money. Given the state of the economy and the widespread public concern about government spending, transit operators seem to have scored with their argument that the administration's handicapped access policy would cost too much.

"The whole question of access to mass transit has become symbolized by a very large dollar sign. Transit operators have worked very hard to equate Section 504 with busting the budget," said Frank Bowe of the American Coalition of Citizens with Disabilities (ACCD), who conceded that the transit operators might be successful this year in their campaign to loosen the existing DOT rules.

But the APTA-supported amendment will have to overcome opposition from Transportation Department officials, who are lobbying strenuously against the change.

DOT Regulations

The target of the attacks by the American Public Transit Association and others is the 1979 Transportation Department regulations on access for the handicapped.

The rules require that:

—"Key" subway stations must be made accessible to the mobility-impaired within 30 years. The requirement applies to the five cities with older facilities that are not now accessible—New York, Boston, Philadelphia, Chicago and Cleveland. Systems built more recently, such as those in Washington, D.C., and San Francisco are already accessible.

Under the "key station" requirement, about 40 percent of subway stops will have to have elevators and ramps so that wheelchair-bound persons can board the trains. Stations that would have to be altered include heavily used stops, transfer points and stations near facilities needed by the handicapped, such as hospitals.

Transit systems could get a waiver of the "key station" mandate if they agreed to provide alternative service, using a combination of buses and vans, that offered equivalent service for the disabled. None of the systems has yet applied for a waiver.

—All new buses must be equipped with lift mechanisms enabling people in wheelchairs to board. Within 10 years, half of all of a transit system's buses in use during rush hour would have to have lifts; in non-rush hours buses with lifts would have to be put into service before buses without lifts.

The regulations also include accessibility requirements for commuter and light rail systems, airports, highway rest stops and intercity trains.

Cost Objections

One of the most important pieces of ammunition in the arsenal of critics of the DOT regulations is a November 1979 report by the Congressional Budget Office (CBO). The report said transit systems would have to spend $6.8 billion—more than twice current annual federal transit spending—over the next 30 years to bring their facilities into compliance.

CBO said alterations in existing rail systems would cost $2.2 billion—twice the Transportation Department's estimate—while another $4.6 billion would have to be spent to adapt buses for wheelchairs, maintain the special equipment and buy additional buses to replace the extra space given over to wheelchair riders.

The wheelchair lifts on buses, in particular, have been an expensive headache to keep in operation. Sensitive pieces of machinery costing up to $20,000, the lifts can jam up easily, particularly in cold weather, and have spilled a number of people in wheelchairs trying to get on the bus. St. Louis, the first big city to install the lifts, has spent more than $600,000 to keep them working.

Comparing the cost of implementing the existing regulations with two alternative approaches—a special van and taxi service for the handicapped, and a plan to provide specially equipped autos to the severely disabled—CBO said the DOT plan would cost more and help fewer people. A van system would cost $4.+ billion and serve about 200,000 more handicapped people, CBO said. The auto plan, while almost as costly as the DOT policy, would serve four times as many severely disabled people, the study said.

Perhaps the most dramatic conclusion of the report was the finding that under the DOT plan, each trip taken by a wheelchair-bound person would cost $38. The van system, by contrast, would cost $7.62 a trip.

DOT Disputes Estimates

The Transportation Department insists that the costs of making transit systems accessible to the handicapped are nowhere near as high as the CBO study would indicate. DOT estimates the 30-year cost of its regulations at $3.2 billion, less than half the CBO figure.

The big difference between the estimates comes from CBO's assumptions that access to bus systems will require heavy maintenance costs and that transit systems will have to buy more buses to make up for lost seating capacity given over to wheelchairs.

DOT officials say maintenance costs will not be as high in the future as they were in St. Louis, where the "first generation" of bus lifts, which had a lot of problems to be worked out, were installed. And they say no additional buses would be needed, since buses seldom operate at full capacity anyway.

Department officials also point out that the costs of making regular transit systems accessible would be one-time costs, while special services expenses would go on forever.

"The special system option very quickly buys a community into a much greater financial difficulty than the long-term solution of accessibility," said Mazziotti.

Whatever the exact costs of accessibility, they would still be far less than the costs of a full-fledged van system operating for three decades, Bowe argued. If all the 2.4 million transportation-disabled people were to sign up for vans just to get to work and back, he said, the cost of that alone would be $8 billion a year.

Low Ridership by Handicapped?

The reason for the extremely high cost-per-trip estimated by CBO, and a central argument made by critics of the DOT regulations, is the belief that very few handicapped people would actually use the bus and subway systems even if all the physical barriers were removed.

Experience with systems that already are accessible tends

to bear out that argument. In the Washington, D.C., area's Metro system, for example, only eight people in wheelchairs now make use of the lifts installed in 90 buses. Other accessible bus systems have had even lower ridership levels.

There are some exceptions. Seattle's bus system has 60 daily wheelchair users. And, according to the latest survey of Washington's Metro rail system, 139 blind, semi-ambulatory and non-ambulatory persons took the subway in one day.

The problem is that the whole world doesn't become accessible to the mobility-impaired person just because the bus has a wheelchair lift. On the most basic level, you can't use a subway elevator if you can't get out of the house and down the street.

"The low ridership is a direct result of the fact that there are other barriers getting to the bus stop," said Helena Barnes of APTA.

Moreover, those aspects of public transportation that often make it aggravating even to the non-disabled—such as lengthy waits in bad weather, or the possibility of crime—are almost insurmountable obstacles to the disabled. It would take an extremely intrepid wheelchair-bound person to attempt to take the bus on a December night in Buffalo, for example.

There are psychological barriers as well. Many handicapped people, explained activist Neil, are very reluctant to make the first attempts to travel on their own. "It is a tremendous fear to have to go out of the security of your own home," she said.

Van Systems Pushed

A system of vans equipped to handle the special needs of the disabled would meet all these problems, say critics of the DOT regulations.

Under van systems, which already are operating in a number of cities, handicapped people arrange in advance to have a van come to their house. The van picks people up at home, delivers them to their appointments, and then takes them home again. Disabled people with jobs can arrange to have the van come every working day.

Thus there is a protective environment for the disabled. There is no problem of getting between home and the transit system, no long waits in bad weather or other risks.

Actually, the merits of a van system don't preclude the idea of making regular transit systems accessible. In an ideal world, there would be both systems, each catering to the special needs of different types of handicapped people.

But the fear of many handicapped activists is that, in the real world, society doesn't have the resources to do both. They worry that their special system might be cut back or closed down if the transit authority has to spend so much money making the buses or trains accessible. "I don't believe there are enough transit dollars to have both," Neil said.

Cleveland Amendment

The APTA and other critics of the DOT regulations are pushing for an amendment to the fiscal 1981–85 mass transit authorization bill (HR 6417) offered in the House Public Works and Transportation Committee by James C. Cleveland (R-N.H.). The amendment would allow exemptions for transit systems that provided equivalent special services for the disabled.

Transit systems could get exemptions if they spent at least 3 percent of their federal transit funds on handicapped transportation, provided special services covering the same area as the regular system, charged users of the special service no more than the fare for the regular system, did not require users of the special services to call up more than 24 hours before they wanted a ride, and developed their plans with participation by the local handicapped community.

No "Separate but Equal" System

Backers of the Transportation Department position respond that reliance on a special system alone simply doesn't meet the non-discrimination requirement of Section 504. They say the meaning of the law runs directly against the idea of a "separate but equal" system reserved for the handicapped.

Lobbyists for the disabled, like the ACCD's Bowe, don't dispute the notion that special services have a role to play in transportation for the handicapped. For some severely disabled people, and in some areas, they say, van transportation is an essential part of the system. What they do disagree with is the notion that vans alone could provide adequate transportation for all disabled people.

"Nobody is saying special services have no place. The difference is over how big a place," Bowe said.

Vans do have their limits. What may work well as a small system, serving several dozen people a day, may not work at all if called upon to move hundreds of people to work, school and shopping each day. Leaving aside questions of cost, the practical aspects of designing van routes for large numbers of people could be extremely difficult, considering the wide variety of locations and schedules the system would have to serve.

"There is a limit to the growth of special services. There is a point beyond which it is not possible to add riders," Bowe argues.

V. NEW WAYS TO SIGHTSEE

EDITOR'S INTRODUCTION

For most Americans, travel is both a necessity and a pleasure. This section describes transportation-as-exercise, surveys leisure, and foresees the future means of transportation for this decade's traveler.

The charms of urban life can be enhanced by trolleys, buses, cable cars, and ferries, suggests a *Changing Times* article, first in the section. It points out places of interest in a dozen cities that can be reached by public transportation at surprising low cost to the traveler. For the urban commuter, the bicycle is another low-cost, pollution-free but vastly underutilized option. Dewey Chiesl, writing in *Bicycling* magazine, discusses the economic, time-saving, and health benefits of two-wheel commuting.

The next ten years may witness a new breed of touring American, dubbed the "80s Traveler" by Horace Sutton. In his *Saturday Review* article, he predicts a world of computers, with supersonic planes, passenger trains that operate by magnetic levitation and travel 250 miles per hour, and battery-operated plastic automobiles. Also predicting the use of electric automobiles, Samuel O'Gorman, in his article entitled "How Will You Get Around in 1991?" from *Senior Scholastic*, foresees a continued American love affair with a more conventional electric car. He pictures the 1991 driver plugging in and recharging at the nearest parking meter.

TROLLEYS, BUSES & FERRIES—GREAT WAYS TO SEE THE SIGHTS[1]

When you're in an unfamiliar city, there are easier ways to get around than driving your own car and cheaper ways

[1] Reprint of staff-written article. *Changing Times*. 35:60+. Ag. '81. Reprinted with permission of CHANGING TIMES Magazine, © 1981 Kiplinger Washington Editors, Inc. This reprint is not altered in any way.

than taking taxis. You can usually join an organized tour of some sort, but consider also the benefits of finding your way on public transportation.

You'll get a different view of the city's life while you travel to the places that interest you, and working out your own itinerary adds to your sense of adventure. Below are some examples of ways to do it.

In *New Orleans* the St. Charles Avenue Streetcar, believed to be the oldest continuously operating streetcar line in the world, is a historic landmark on wheels. Start at the edge of the French Quarter and travel along the boulevard-wide St. Charles Avenue through the Garden District, University Section and Audubon Park, passing mansions built by planters, cotton traders and rivermen.

The trip takes about 45 minutes one way, but you can stop at museums, the zoo, shops and restaurants. A $4 ticket is valid all day; streetcars pass almost every ten minutes. *The Streetcar Guide to Uptown New Orleans* (TransiTour, Inc.; $5 paperback) tells all about it and is available at most New Orleans bookstores and the Streetcar Store, which is at 111 St. Charles Ave.

In *San Diego* the first red streetcar on the first U.S. streetcar line built in 20 years pulled out of the historic Santa Fe railway depot on July 1 [1981]. It's known as the "Tijuana Trolley" because the 15½-mile ride ends in Tijuana, Mexico.

In *San Francisco* the cable cars clanking up and down steep streets are the most famous streetcars in the world. Their ten miles of track lead to such destinations as Fisherman's Wharf, Ghirardelli Square and part of the Golden Gate National Recreation Area. The Cable Car Barn at Washington and Mason streets displays early transit relics and the actual wheels pulling the cables.

For a 50-cent fare with transfer privileges ($1 for an unlimited Sunday pass) you can ride on the Municipal Railway's 700-mile network of streetcars, buses and cable cars. Or take BART (Bay Area Rapid Transit) the modern subway linking downtown San Francisco with Oakland and the East Bay. Or travel with commuters across the bay on the new ferries that go to Sausalito, Tiburon and Larkspur.

In *Pittsburgh* the historic Duquesne Incline is one of two

remaining funiculars in the city, operating since 1877 and rescued from threatened extinction by local citizens in 1963. For 40 cents one way you ride to the 400-foot-high summit, where the observation deck provides spectacular vistas of the Golden Triangle, Pittsburgh's downtown area.

In *Seattle* try the modern ferry fleet that serves two different routes. Each ferry has a restaurant, observation deck and glassed-in viewing area for use when the weather turns bad.

Fares vary with length of trip, passengers per vehicle and whether you're bicycling or walking. For a bargain, take the walk-on, 30-minute excursion to Winslow on Bainbridge Island or the 55-minute crossing of fjordlike Rich Passage to Bremerton (where the USS *Missouri* is berthed). The excursion fare is only $1.70 round trip and allows up to five hours on shore.

Or you can ferry across Puget Sound and drive to the Olympic Peninsula, ocean beaches and island state parks.

The all-day summer trip from Anacortes, 83 miles north of Seattle, winds north through the San Juan Islands to Sidney, British Columbia, where convenient bus connections are available to downtown Victoria, the province's capital, 17 miles away.

In *Portland,* Ore., virtually all bus routes begin and end at the redeveloped mall in the heart of the city—an 11-block area landscaped with sculpture, fountains, walkways and benches.

Take the No. 63 bus to the International Rose Gardens, Japanese Gardens, Hoyt Arboretum, Oregon Museum of Science and Industry and the Washington Park Zoo. Or take the No. 53 to Forest Park for a hike on the Wildwood Trail, then return on the No. 63.

In *Honolulu* board "TheBus," No. 52, at Ala Moana shopping center near Waikiki Beach for a good introduction to the city. The four-hour, 50-cent ride around Oahu passes major attractions on the north coast (including the Polynesian Cultural Center, Kahuku Sugar Mill and Wahiawa Botanical Gardens), and the Arizona Memorial at Pearl Harbor on its way back into Honolulu.

In *New York* there are two Culture Bus loops; one covers

midtown and upper Manhattan and the other covers lower Manhattan and Brooklyn. They operate weekends and most holidays, stopping at the front doors of virtually all major cultural institutions and tourist attractions. Cost: $1.75 per loop, no matter how many times you get on and off.

The subway system provides access to museums, theaters, scenic attractions and architectural landmarks throughout four of New York's five boroughs. For a 60¢ [75¢] token you can ride from the Bronx Zoo to Coney Island and Brighton Beach on the Atlantic Ocean. The subways run mostly above ground when outside the downtown area. You reach the fifth borough, Staten Island, via the ferry ride from the Battery at the tip of Manhattan, crossing the bustling harbor with close views of the Statue of Liberty and Ellis Island. This mini cruise costs only 25 cents round trip.

In *Philadelphia* there is a culture bus, too, shuttling up and down Benjamin Franklin Parkway with on-off privileges. It's designed to resemble an old-fashioned, open-air trolley and makes 22 stops on a 17-mile round trip. The $4.50 fare includes discount admissions to such attractions as the Philadelphia Art Museum, the zoo and restored colonial mansions in Fairmount Park.

In *London* one good way to see the major sights is on a two-hour bus tour run by the transport authority. It covers the Tower of London, Westminster Abbey, Trafalgar Square, and other spots of interest to tourists. There is no guide aboard, but you get a free illustrated map. No advance booking is needed either; hop aboard at Victoria Station, Piccadilly Circus or Marble Arch. The fare is £2.40 (about $5.20).

You can also look at London from atop a double-decker bus. No. 11 and No. 12 are best for landmark viewing at less than a dollar a ride. And there is a cut-rate "go-as-you-please" pass for unlimited travel on buses and the underground (subway) for your choice of three, four or seven days (or the "Central Tube Rover" for one day of underground alone).

In *Amsterdam* modern, soundless, comfortable streetcars take you almost everywhere you'd want to go: the Rijksmuseum, Concertgebouy, Rembrandtsplein and across the canals. Most routes start and end at Central Station. The fare is one

Dutch guilder (about 40 cents), but vending machines at every trolley stop sell six-ticket packets at even lower cost— and you can use the same ticket as many times as you want within 45 minutes after it has been stamped. Central Station, incidentally, is also the starting point of low-cost day excursions to such points as The Hague, Rotterdam and Brussels on fast, frequent and dependable trains.

In *Hong Kong* you might start from Kowloon and ride across the harbor aboard the fabled Star Ferry for about 10 cents in first class or 6 cents in second class. Hop on the hill-climbing cable car to Victoria Peak, a ride that costs 40 cents and treats you to spectacular vistas of the harbor and city. Then descend via a bus and aged, creaky streetcar, for about 15 to 20 cents. For a modest $1.25 you can take a one-hour ferry ride to mountainous Lantau, Hong Kong's largest island, or Cheung Chau, the island without a single motor vehicle, where transportation is by bicycle or shank's mare.

BICYCLES FOR TRANSPORTATION[2]

The commuter is typically tired and in a hurry, anxious to get to work on time. He travels the same route every day by habit and is angered by the slightest delay. Extra minutes enroute are automatically multiplied by 240 working days a year and thought of in terms of days wasted sitting behind a wheel. The commuter needs a change of pace. He can find it by bicycling to work.

The most often raised objections to commuting by bicycle concern time and distance. Let's consider ten miles as the maximum comfortable range for commuting by bike and 12 miles per hour a speed that anyone could maintain. How does this compare with average distances and speeds when commuting by car?

[2] Reprint of article by Dewey Chiesl. *Bicycling.* Mr. '77. p 59–62. Reprinted from the March 1977 issue of *Bicycling* Magazine with permission from Rodale Press, Inc., Copyright 1977.

The Chicago Area Transportation Study (CATS) conducted a survey of travel characteristics in an eight-county area around Chicago in 1970. Data was taken for one weekday on mode, purpose and time of day. Home interviews and roadside surveys were used. Also in 1970 a similar study was done in the Minneapolis/St. Paul area by the Transportation Planning Program. Both studies were compared with a previous study done in the same area about 15 years earlier.

It is interesting to note that although the number of trips increased significantly from the mid-fifties (from 2.9 million in 1958 to 4.6 million auto trips in 1970 in the TPP study), average commuting distance increased only slightly, by about one mile in Chicago. Therefore, we can consider the 1970 figures to be stable for some time.

In the Chicago area the average automobile commuting distance was 6.3 miles. The average speed was 15.0 mph. In the Twin Cities area it was 4.9 at 22.1 mph (nonfreeway) and 9.7 miles at 29.5 mph (freeway). Arbitrarily averaging these three pairs of numbers yields an average distance of 6.9 miles at 22 mph. Comparing this to the bicycle averages we have: a car traveling 6.9 miles at 22 mph requires 18.8 minutes; a bicycle traveling 6.9 miles at 12 mph requires 34.5 minutes. In other words, it takes the bicyclist another 15 minutes to travel the 6.9 miles.

For the purist who argues that the time saved by car is too important to sacrifice, consider this: average enroute times and door-to-door times may differ more widely for the motorist than the cyclist. The automobile must be started, warmed up and the windows cleared before it can be driven. At the destination a parking place must be searched for and located and then the distance to the office walked at four miles an hour. All these activities could easily consume the motorist's 15-minute advantage.

The bicyclist has no such problems. He rides off immediately and parks quickly at work, either nearby or by carrying his bike inside with him. Thus a more accurate comparison is based on door-to-door times which would seem to be very close between the bicycle and the automobile.

Average speeds and distances, though, are not the primary selling points of the bicycle. A bicycle is economical to operate. Conversely, few people realize how much their cars cost them. *Changing Times* recently printed this startling item: "Buying a new car? Total cost: $17,878.96." This sum was computed for a standard size 1976 car driven 10,000 miles per year for ten years. It includes gas, maintenance, insurance, parking, tolls and taxes. That same amount would buy 40 ten-speed bicycles and provide for their maintenance for ten years (assuming the bike cost $150 and upkeep was $30 per year).

The American Automobile Association (AAA) published a pamphlet entitled *Your Driving Costs*, 1975, which further substantiates the high costs of owning and operating a car. An automobile has two types of costs, according to the pamphlet, variable and fixed. The variable portion is dependent on how much the car is used and includes gas, oil, maintenance and tires. Fixed costs generally remain constant over a year despite how much the car is driven. For a 1975 Chevrolet Chevelle, eight-cylinder, the variable cost per mile is 6.45 cents. Fixed costs are $1,186 per year. If 10,000 miles are driven in a year, the total cost per mile is:

$0.0645/mi 10,000 mi/yr = $645 + $1,186 = $1,831/yr
$1,831/yr/ 10,000 mi/yr = $0.183/mi (18.3 cents/mi)

On the other hand, a bicycle that sells for $150 and costs $30 each year to maintain costs only $45 each year if used for ten years. Let's assume that the bicycle is used exclusively for commuting to work six miles or about 3,000 miles per year. The cost per mile becomes:

$45/yr/ 3,000 mi/yr = $0.015/mi

or 1.5 cents per mile (less if the bike is used for noncommuting trips as well). Compare this with 18.3 cents per mile for the car. Even the so-called economical cars are expensive. According to the AAA pamphlet, a compact auto costs 16.2 cents per mile and a subcompact 15.1 cents per mile.

After a few years several thousand dollars can be saved by bicycling to work. However, if a car is just sitting idle in the garage, it still costs the owner about a thousand dollars each year in fixed costs. For more economy it is best not to own the car and rely on other means of transportation when it is undesirable to bicycle.

Financially, the bicycle is far superior to the car, and this advantage is likely to improve since automobile costs are soaring. Bob Sheldon of the Minneapolis AAA estimates that the cost per mile of a car will increase some 10 to 15 percent each year. He blames rising insurance rates, cost of repairs and high initial selling prices.

Rationally, the bicycle is an excellent alternative to the automobile for most commuters. Yet people are still tied emotionally to their cars. This fact became evident from three studies conducted by Barton Aschman Associates, Minneapolis. In 1974 they assembled data on bicycle usage in Pennsylvania, Tennessee and the District of Columbia. Barton Aschman found that of the 40 percent of Americans who bicycle, only 15 percent of their trips were for utility purposes. A utility trip has a specific, nonrecreational purpose such as shopping, personal business or commuting. Of all the utility trips, commuting to work comprised only 20 percent, or three percent of all bicycle usage. Why do so few bicyclists pedal to work?

Two important clues were apparent from the Barton Aschman studies: first, 50 percent of all U.S. bicyclists are under 16; and second, the frequency of bicycle trips drops sharply at age 16.

Besides attraction to the opposite sex, the acquisition of one's driver's license is the most critical influence in the life of a 16-year-old. Driving an automobile becomes a symbol of adulthood, and the bicycle is put aside as a childhood toy. Several years later when the glitter has begun to fade and the young adult has experienced rush-hour traffic, emptied his wallet buying a tank of gas, and generally found aiming two tons of steel and plastic unexciting, it's too late. By then he has forgotten the utility, economy and, sadly, the joys of bicycling. This is unfortunate since there is a childlike sense of freedom and excitement in bicycling that would help brighten the day of many serious-minded adult commuters.

James M. Barrie, British novelist and playwright, author of *Peter Pan*, had definite feelings about adulthood. After

Peter Pan opened in London in 1904, critics wondered why Barrie had created such a masterpiece solely about youth. Barrie's reply was, "Oh that we were boys and girls all our lives . . . for nothing that happens after we are twelve matters very much."

Perhaps the greatest advantages of the bicycle for commuting cannot be measured; yet these are exactly the reasons that would eliminate much grumbling from the automobile commuter.

The car provides a degree of freedom over mass transit that people prefer. Yet the bicyclist enjoys a further degree of freedom over the motorist. The bicycling commuter can leave when he wants and travel a variety of routes. He can enjoy the solitude of empty roads and the beauty of scenic routes neglected by the motorist because they are too slow. Another freedom in bicycling is having no speed limit. A bicyclist on his way to work isn't frustrated by slow-moving traffic or backups at traffic lights. A cyclist always travels as fast as he cares to. He has a much greater range of speeds to choose from and usually travels slower than his maximum. A cyclist is more inclined to stop for a while to look at something interesting. He is part of the environment and feels it.

A growing acceptance of the bicycle in America may provide part of the solution to the commuter's woes. But how can commuters make the switch from car to bicycle? Oliver Towne, a columnist for the *St. Paul Dispatch* and an avid commuter at 56, probably gives the most succinct advice. When asked how someone could get started bicycling to work, he replied, "Try it."

80s TRAVELER: HIS LIFE AND FUTURE TIMES[3]

It was spring in California, and the big new airplane bearing the blue, white, and red colors of British Airways was poised at the end of the runway at Lockheed's Palmdale

[3] Reprint of article by Horace Sutton, writer. *Saturday Review*. 7:20–4. Ja. 5, '80.

plant. Captain John D'Arcy, the airline's chief TriStar pilot, flipped on the intercom and told his passengers that this was not merely a delivery flight but a novel voyage. He would throw the switches that would turn the plane over to the computers, and that mechanism would take it to London 5,500 miles away. With that, the Dash 500, as this new version of the L-1011 is called, rolled down the runway. Nine hours and 35 minutes later it descended to an automatic landing at Heathrow Airport. Not a human hand had been laid on the controls, which had been automatically adjusted through the flight for direction and altitude as well as for maximum fuel economy.

Was the flight of the Dash 500 piloted by those same computers that have been snarling department store bills, dispatching unwarranted dunning notices, losing reservations, and performing other horrors chalked up during the Seventies to that horde of faceless maladroits called Computer Error?

Well, er, yes, but the mechanical mind, having reached its maturity, having been preened, tutored, and otherwise souped up, may well turn this decade into the Automated Age. On behalf of that hopeful peregrinator, 80s Traveler, the device will, aside from piloting planes, guide high-speed trains, make possible the flight of the space shuttle that is expected to ignite the thinking of aeronautical designers, and tilt everybody toward an ultimate age of rocket propulsion. India in an hour, and all that.

The computer brain in this decade can be made to store and display data on a selection of vacations that fit the needs and style of 80s Traveler. After all, if the campuses are already offering computer dating, why not computer travel agents able to match in an instant the right place in the world to the personality and pocketbook of the client?

If 80s Traveler is to enjoy the luxury of high-speed trains roaring from city center to city center on retina-popping time schedules, it will only be because the computer keeps an electric eye on the engineer's cabin. In other forms, the computer brain will take over the operation of automobiles to prevent accidents and ensure economical fuel consumption.

It will also record restaurant orders in hotels, tote up your bill and apply it to your credit card. As magic eyes go, it is the most significant development since the employment of the double whammy.

Hotels

For 80s Traveler, "the hotel," in the words of Curt Strand, president of Hilton International, "will play an even more important role as an oasis of repose, relaxation, convenience, and comfort, a sanctuary from the hassle of getting from here to there." To Charles Bell, his executive vice-president, this will mean a world of hoteldom in which 80s Traveler, coming down to breakfast, will order two fried eggs, an order punched into a computer terminal and delivered printed to the chef. Meanwhile, it will also print a check, charge the amount to Traveler's room, and advise the purchasing agent that there are two less eggs in the inventory.

The vast hotel informations systems will eliminate all sorts of expensive tedium. Weary after a long day, 80s Traveler, returning to his hotel and eager to get the key and go up to bed, will not be required to wait until the night auditor is finished posting the cost of a club sandwich and beer to Room 342.

Says Joseph Kordsmeier of Hyatt's mushrooming, world-spanning chain, "The secret of the decade is communication. Who runs the reservation system runs the world."

Even now, the guest who makes a booking but fails to arrive by 6 P.M. might well find his reservation cancelled. The hotel presumes he will not appear. The 80s Traveler, however, will find that the omnipresent, irrepressible computer will have its electronic mitts on his credit card. No-shows who fail to cancel will find the hotel charge on their monthly credit card bill.

Charges incurred in assorted corners of a large hotel—bar, pool, dining room, sauna—will all filter into a central computer. In Europe, says Hans Sternik of Pan Am's Inter-Continental chain, "the computer must be supported by a back-up energy system." But that is a small price to pay. The night clerk, once distracted, now has time to give the guest the correct room key. Moreover, in Sternik's system, with 80 hotels to control in over 48 countries, satellites will deliver balance sheets. It will be theoretically possible for Sternik to sit in his office in the Pan Am building, high above the East River, look at the printout, and note that schnitzel moves better than goulash in Kuala Lumpur.

In a world that has become less safe and more suspicious, hotels have been obligated to put more muscle in their security to prevent theft, assault, and even kidnapping. Once inside the hotel, 80s Traveler can rest assured electronic systems will work to protect his possessions and his person.

Inter-Continental has returned to putting peep holes in its hotel-room doors. Moreover, it is looking at electric sensors that will turn off the lights when you leave, and even reveal a presence in the room when your key is still in your bag.

Hilton, Hyatt, and others are contemplating discarding keys in favor of an electronic lock device. In a new system, a guest will be issued a card prepared by a computer console fitted out with a security printer. The first time the guest inserts the card in the door lock he cancels the previous key, and from then on the door will open only with his key. If the computer console becomes inoperative, the locks and guest key will still work. A grand master programmer is kept in the safe.

Although the *art* of hotelkeeping will be smoothed, both for hotelier and for guests in the Eighties, what of the hotels themselves?

Hilton will build a string of modern hotels in Brazil which it is calling Brasiltons, each with a coffee shop that doubles as the grill and restaurant. They are to be built at a third of the cost of a luxury hotel. With the plan set for Brazil, which may blossom, at last, as a traveler's favored destination, Hilton is tooling up for a similar string across Europe. It won't be alone. Inter-Continental has plans for four or five Forum hotels that will offer basic comfort and cost 35 percent less than deluxe inns.

The format for the Forum hotels, to be sprinkled across

Europe and the Middle East, calls for one restaurant and one bar. Guests will take their own laundry to a shop in the lobby, and while they won't be asked to drop it in a Laundromat, they will be required to pick it up themselves at night. Such curtailed services may offset the high ground prices that exist against the dollar in many European countries. They will also help bring the hotel cost in line with reduced air fares that by themselves are attracting a new class of traveler. Often a new nationality of traveler. In 1966 half the guests in Hilton hotels were Americans; now that number is down to one in four.

Eighties Traveler, in Curt Strand's view, will be "less homogeneous, which means a hotel will have to cater to diverse tastes." Hilton's new Vista International hotels in the United States will have international hotel features—currency exchange, concierge, and multilingual personnel. If accustomed to cultivated tastes, 80s Traveler will not want for stylish comfort. Hyatt has plans for a super deluxe jewel-box hotel in Chicago that will extract a minimum tariff of $125 a day. It will take no group business, no conventions, and no connected band larger than a board of directors. At the same time, the company will unveil the Grand Hyatt New York, a 1,400-room redo of the Commodore Hotel, next August. Acknowledging that the traveler of the Eighties will be a diverse character of varying needs, Hyatt is also adding to its Regency Hotel in Chicago more than 1,000 rooms to serve four distinct areas: trade show, convention, regular transit business, and super-deluxe VIP.

Ships

As 70s Traveler learned, ships are now floating hotels. In the Eighties, every ingenious maritime ploy will be tried to offset soaring fuel costs as well as general inflation. "For the Eighties passenger," says Warren Titus, president of Royal Viking Lines and former head of the Cruise Line Association, "this may mean we will cut down on steaming at sea, reschedule to reduce speeds, and spend more time in port." It also means a continuing search for an alternate propellant.

Ship lines hope to learn from the experience gained by the navy's use of nuclear-powered vessels.

The seagoing 80s Traveler will find less of a choice in rooms. New ships are using a modular design in which most rooms, except those near the bow and the stern, are standard size. Modular-constructed ships are cheaper to build, easier to market, and readily enlarged with the addition of a midsection, a popular modality even now. "The only technological advance I've heard of," Titus says, "is a catamaran hull design that would give you a much more favorable rectangular platform on which to build your 'hotel' structure. The shallower draft would allow more speed at the same fuel consumption." All that is still a drawing board dream. The ships being planned now are in the 1,000-passenger-and-up class, with no ships the size or style of the *QE II* or the *France* in view in the next decade.

Trains

The Germans are perfecting a train that operates by magnetic levitation. Maglev, as 80s Traveler may learn to call it, is not to be confused with riding an air cushion. It is not a version of a hovercraft, which does not adapt to terrestrial transport, except in remote swamp areas or tundra. Nor has it to do with rockets, which have been tried, but produced unconscionable pollution.

Working in successive trials that started in the Sixties, two German companies, Krauss-Maffei and Messerschmitt, funded by the German Federal Ministry of Transport, have produced a railroad car that will wrap itself around a single-beam elevated guideway. The train will be operable at ground level and, for that matter, underground. In unpopulated areas it could be constructed just high enough for strolling caribou and moose to pass underneath. The guideway doesn't cut up the countryside in the manner of railroads, and is less expensive to build than a conventional high-speed railroad.

Eighties Traveler could use this Transrapid system traveling at up to 250 miles an hour between Dallas and Houston, Washington and New York, or Los Angeles and San Francisco. The distance from Munich to Hamburg, covered by air in an hour and a quarter today, would take 80s Traveler, en route to ski in Bavaria or sail in the Baltic, two hours and a half, stops included, with Transrapid. But the maglev system connects city center to city center. To the air time one has to add three hours of transit time and waiting time.

Abroad in France, 80s Traveler will find the Paris-Lyon and Geneva-Marseille runs served by a high-speed electric train capable of running at 160 to 180 mph. It will cut hours off the present schedules. By mid-decade, France expects to have 25 million passengers, many of them former automobile travelers, riding on its $2 billion railway.

In this country the Budd Company is showing a self-propelled diesel-energized railway car for possible short hauls between Boston and Cape Cod or Philadelphia and Atlantic City. Depending upon the configuration, the Budd vehicle can carry 109 passengers on a dry car, or 86 if a bar is installed. Operated by one engineer from either end, it can attain speeds of 120 miles an hour and is an ideal people-mover for resort travel. In Vermont it could run to ski resorts on unused tracks. It could fetch passengers from San Francisco to Reno, or run on the old Chessie tracks to the Greenbrier.

Cars

Behind the wheel, 80s Traveler will be both protected and advised by a system of tiny electronic chips tied to sonar and radar, which will warn him of an oncoming car in the wrong lane, a slick road ahead. If there is need to pump the brakes carefully rather than risk hydroplaning by slamming them on, computers can be programmed to take the braking operation away from the heavy foot of the driver and activate more cautionary measures. Moreover, electronic chips will compute the most efficient speeds to conserve gas.

Stanford Research Institute in Menlo Park, California, sees gasoline production reaching a peak only two years into the Eighties, and declining after that. But the shortage of gas won't leave 80s Traveler carless and immobile. According to Stanford's seers the family car will not be called upon to serve as the dray horse of all labor. Rather, there may be a wider variety of vehicles—motorbike and electronic cars for short-distance driving and larger cars for longer trips—many of them more likely to be leased than owned.

Eighties Traveler will find himself driving a car made of heavy-duty plastic, a vehicle that may not be smaller, but will be lighter and therefore require less petrol. Lighter cars are also more adaptable to battery power.

Although automobile companies guard their secrets the way super powers guard their contingency plans, Ford, near decade's end, stimulated public nosiness by showing some television commercials that talked about such futuristics as a ceramic turbine gas engine that gets 30 percent better mileage than a standard engine of the same size. Ford's engineers were testing, the company revealed, a hybrid vehicle that runs on battery power at speeds up to 20 mph, then goes over to gasoline. On its boards, too, is a four-cylinder Mustang that is "turbocharged" to produce the same power as an eight-cylinder car.

Planes

The limitations and the cost of fuel have had a marked effect on the traditional move, decade by decade, into speedier methods of air transport. The Eighties are the first post-World War II decade that will not stoke the wanderlust with a major aeronautic advancement. Ticking off the major changes since the war's end 35 years ago, Dan Colussy, Pan Am's president, is almost rueful. "We went from pistons to the first jets," he says, "then to fan jets and to wide bodies." Later the technology of supersonic travel was introduced by the British-French Concorde and its Soviet counterpart. In less than 50 years man moved from an average transatlantic Zeppelin speed of 59.7 mph in 1928 to a Concorde speed of 1,046 miles an hour in 1976. No such jump is likely for 80s Traveler. "There is not going to be any dramatic airplane technology introduced," Colussy says, and his flat statement is borne out by airplane manufacturers, most of whom will be refining planes already in use. Eighties Traveler might be seated in a stretched-out version of a plane he already knows, a cold comfort if he is in business class paying full tourist fare, or in third class paying discount fare. Seats will be closer together and may not recline as far.

Boeing will lengthen the upper deck lounge and add a piece to the midsection of the 747 body. A passenger service specialist for Boeing, Fred Schroeder, says "The real estate on an airplane is more valuable than the real estate in Manhattan." Two inches may be cut from the distance between seats, but he insists there will be the "same shin room."

The 747 could be stretched to take 750 people, but such a quantum jump seems unlikely in this decade. A 500-seat airplane seems more probable. Some airlines will emphasize first class, but others will drop it altogether. Japan Air Lines's decision to put berths between North America and the Orient—a throwback to the Stratocruisers of the late Fifties—has prompted Philippine Airlines to have them put in. Pan American is installing Sleeperette seats on all its wide-bodied planes, Colussy says, even if it means giving up its popular upper deck dining room service.

Beginning in 1982 Boeing will also produce a wide-bodied twinjet 767 to carry 211 passengers for United, American, and Delta. Pacific Western of Canada and Air Canada, as well as All Nippon will use the two-aisle plane.

Lockheed's Dash 500 will save British Airways—so that airline's engineering department estimates—$60,000 a year in fuel costs on each aircraft. Pan Am is using the plane on its Latin America division starting this year, and future deliveries go to AeroPeru, Delta, and British West Indian Airways.

All this airplane expansion calls for using derivatives of crude oil, a commodity that will reach its peak of world production—depending upon whose survey one chooses to believe—somewhere between 1990 and 2000. As an alternative, Lockheed's thinkers are fascinated by the prospect of using hydrogen. Willis Hawkins, senior vice-president of Lockheed says, "The hydrogen airplane represents the biggest single step in aircraft efficiency we have ever experienced . . . more important than the step we made when we moved from reciprocating engines to jet engines."

Hawkins sees an airplane with a huge thermos bottle for a fuselage to hold the liquid hydrogen. Seats would be fitted fore and aft. All that are needed to make this fuel are power and water. The power could be nuclear, hydroelectric, solar, or coal. Of the world's airports, 16 account for 38 percent of the traffic traveling over 1,500 nautical miles. Hawkins proposes manufacturing liquid hydrogen, or LH_2, at these terminals and storing it there. By the end of this decade the passenger demand generated at these 16 terminals could support 370 passenger transports, each equipped with 400 seats. Says Hawkins, "It looks to us as though airplanes will be in serious trouble as early as 1985. We might all stagger along for another 10 years, then build a new transport, but we could convert one in three or four years."

More audaciously, Lockheed peers far ahead and sees a hydrogen-fueled plane that would provide power and at the same time cool the sides of the plane, making possible a hypersonic craft whose body could be made of titanium or aluminum or a combination of the two. A turbojet would lift the plane from runway to a speed of about 600 mph. At that point the supersonic combustion ramjet engine, called SCRAM, would cut in, ultimately boosting the speed to Mach 6, six times the speed of sound at sea level, or 4,000 miles an hour.

That would mean Los Angeles–Tokyo in two hours, 18 minutes, or New York–London in just about one hour. NASA is playing with that study now, planning an aircraft to cruise at over 100,000 feet, at which altitude the sonic boom would be dissipated before it reached earth.

Such a prospect may not seem so awesome once the space shuttle program gets under way, this year or next. The shuttle will have wings, and while resembling, more or less, a conventional aircraft, it will land at existing airports. This NASA project should inspire aeronautical engineers, for if humans can rendezvous in space and return to earth, landing at an airport, why would it not be possible, using the same technology, to girdle the earth in a tenth of the time it now takes?

Crystal-ball gazers at Stanford Research Institute talk of rocket travel by the 2020s.

Considering all these flights of fancy, what ever happened to the SST, 80s Traveler might ask? David Raphael, a senior economist in SRI's International Business Intelligence Program, foresees no more than 10 SSTs in operation through the 1990s. Naggingly persistent rumors put the number at less than that, for although the supersonic Concorde has proved to be far less of an environmental bugaboo than the pre-flight hysteria led people to believe, it arrived at an inopportune time, when the cost of petroleum turned the world economy upside down. It carried too few seats to permit its economic success.

Some 15 years from now, 90s Traveler may well find himself flying a U.S.-made SST, a large titanium airplane that will zoom the stratosphere at Mach 3, or better than 2,000 miles an hour. Concerned with keeping their own airframe industry alive, the Europeans, then, may well reenter the fray to produce an enlarged, competing Concorde.

Airports

Eighties Traveler will be the beneficiary of moves being made to reduce the size of airports, shorten those overland hikes to plane-side, and abolish ticketing at terminals and even baggage handling.

Before his time is out 80s Traveler may well see the day when he can have a ticket written in his office to be billed on his own credit card. If the distance between the check-in point and plane-side can be reduced to a sensible distance, he could carry his bag aboard.

Planners are looking for airport sites that can be reached by all means of transport—rail, bus, and car. Much is made of Mirabel, technically the world's largest airport, which sits outside Montreal, a 45-minute to one-hour trip from the Central Station by bus and a $25 (Canadian) fare by taxi. The terminal, long and narrow, is designed as a pass-through for departing travelers with the maximum walking distance cut to 130 paces. Passenger transfer vehicles operating from 38 docks take passengers directly to planes, a system first tried at Washington's Dulles Airport.

Mayor Jean Drapeau of Montreal, an experienced dreamer or a brilliant visionary depending upon how you see him (he brought Montreal Expo '67 and the Olympics of 1976), views Mirabel as an airport that will one day handle a third of all the traffic in eastern North America. He envisions rapid transport linking Mirabel and New York City.

Eighties traveler, roaming the surrealist sections of downtown Los Angeles, may find himself traveling from the glass cylinders of the Bonaventure Hotel to the theater aboard a People Mover, an electric, automatically controlled transit system running on an overhead guideway above downtown streets. Scheduled to open in mid-1983, the People Mover expects to be carrying better than 72,000 passengers a day by decade's end, many of them riding between downtown hotels and the convention center.

No rare or endangered species, 80s Traveler will number a mighty mass of one billion peregrinators, or so the United Nations estimates. A magazine called the *Futurist* wonders whether travel will be the world's biggest industry by the 21st century. It cites the need to escape from modern work, which is "highly specialized, fragmented, lacking autonomy, and repetitious," if not downright routine. "Travel," it says, "satisfies the need to escape." Moreover, the traveler is not only escaping work, but is escaping the so-called "compulsive time"—maintaining one's home or just preparing for work, an ethic first advanced by Henri Lefevre in his book, *Everyday Life in the Modern World.*

One decade ago, a trade magazine called *Travel Weekly* gathered a group of social scientists at Princeton in a series of seminars chaired by the late Dr. Margaret Mead. What the group found was a world of new hotels, faster planes, and the accessibility of exotic places, and more significantly a change in people themselves. The postwar babies who came of age in the Seventies shared a new concern for themselves and a deep desire to live a richer, fuller life beyond the rewards of work. They became the 70s Traveler.

As their decade drew to a close, a similar seminar, spon-

sored by Boeing and *Travel Weekly,* was held at a travel industry convention in Munich. Now the panel revealed it had
found out that last year more than half of all American adults
took at least one 200-mile trip that included air fare or paid
accommodations—a jump of 16 million people in one year.
All told, Americans took 276 million trips, an increase of 66
percent. Some of that explosion came from the greater number of working women with more money to travel and more
need to escape from stress. Social researcher Daniel Yankelo-
vich and Jock Elliott, chairman of Ogilvy and Mather, examined the social motivations. Most of us had grown up with a
sense of self-denial, they said. Spending money on one's self
was against the ethic of the time. One's job and one's home
were the important aspects of one's life, and travel played a
marginal role. But new values were born in the Sixties and
they spread in the Seventies to the rest of the population. We
shifted away from self-denial and began to enrich ourselves
by expanding our horizons. Travel has ceased to be marginal.
It is no longer a luxury, but part of a life plan. We may need
to make some cutbacks—pare a three-week trip to a fort-
night, a winter's week in the sun or the snow to a long week-
end. Those are but economic adjustments. There is an accepted need to escape, a right to escape in the face of stress.
The shift from self-denial to spending on oneself may well be
what life will be all about for that dauntless dasher, the 80s
Traveler.

HOW WILL YOU GET AROUND IN 1991?[4]

What will you be driving ten years from now?

"AN ELECTRIC CAR!" was a frequent response ten years ago.
It can still be heard today.

Many Americans have, however, become disillusioned
with predictions of a future based on exotic car designs—

[4] Article by Samuel O'Gorman. *Senior Scholastic.* 114:8–11. O. 16, '81. By permission of the publisher.

electric, magnetic, hydrogen-fueled, air-cushioned, etc. Instead, they consider that most of us will be driving cars similar to those on the roads right now. The 1991 models will probably be smaller, lighter, much more expensive, and pack less horsepower than present cars. And Gasahol (a mixture of gasoline and alcohol) will probably be available at every "gas" station. Though long-distance driving may decline, the average American will probably travel more than he does now—combining air travel with car rentals for local use.

Of course there are people, particularly those in metropolitan areas, who disagree with these predictions. They respond to the "what-will-you-be driving?" question with a question: "What makes you sure that most of us will be driving anything by 1991?"

People living in urban/suburban areas tend to have a gloomy view of the future of transportation. Roads in their areas are often crumbling, congested and inadequate. And prospects for improvement seem dim. Many communities have neither the space nor the funds for new roads. They frequently don't even have enough funds for adequate road repairs. Added to this is the fact that parking in downtown areas can be close to impossible. And rush-hour traffic is frequently nightmarish.

"Getting around is no snap—not with an air-traffic controllers' strike, crumbling roads, crowded trains"

Not only has the difficulty of getting around increased in urban/suburban areas, so too has the cost. The share of personal income that must go to pay for transportation has climbed sharply in recent years. Now, according to the U.S. Department of Commerce, about 15 cents out of every dollar spent goes for transportation. And, unless some great change occurs, the cost share for transportation is likely to go on increasing.

People are also finding that "getting away from it all" is becoming increasingly more difficult. Air travel, once a great adventure, has become a hassle for many people.

Airports have explosively expanded far beyond the outlines of the original plans. In most metropolitan areas, airports are huge, impersonal, bewildering, crowded most of the time, and frequently uncomfortable. Getting around within a major airport can often be quite a challenge because parking lots, access roads and the terminal buildings of various airlines may be scattered over a large area. As one observer put it, many metropolitan airports have in recent years taken on most of the problems of metropolitan centers. These include crime, confusion and congestion.

The congestion problems of airports extend to the sky above. A jetliner having completed a flight from another metropolitan area in two hours may spend nearly an hour in a holding pattern—flying around waiting for its turn to land.

Long before the air-traffic controllers' strike (August, 1981), crowding of the airways and the difficulty of controlling air traffic over metropolitan areas were considered major problems. And many experts believed that such air traffic difficulties would eventually limit the number of flights that could go in and out of certain airports. In their view, such limitations would further increase the cost of air travel and restrict its use.

Soaring expenses, such as a 900 percent increase in the price of jet fuel over the past ten years had already led to sharp increases in air fares. Despite the publicity given to certain discount fare offerings, the overall cost of air travel increased by 30 percent between July, 1980 and July, 1981. As a result, many people have been discouraged from using air transport for vacations and visits. The airlines are now finding that an ever-increasing share of their business comes from business travelers.

The air-traffic controllers' strike and the subsequent reorganization of the air-traffic control system have compounded these difficulties. Delays, uncertainties, and the fear of potential danger in the sky discouraged many people from air travel. At the same time, delays, uncertainties, cancellations, and loss of potential passengers sharply decreased the airlines' profits. The air-traffic controllers' strike forced millions of people onto the highways and onto other transportation systems that were in many cases already overcrowded and quite unprepared for the additional load.

U.S. News and World Report of August 31, 1981 summed up the situation this way:

> Getting around is no snap any more—not with an air-traffic controllers' strike, crumbling highways and crowded bus and train systems. . . . Whether it's by car or air, travel is becoming a bigger hassle.

If travel by car or air is such a hassle, some people say, shouldn't we improve such alternate means of transportation as trains and buses? After all, they argue, buses and trains are more energy efficient than cars and planes.

A number of transportation experts disagree with this. A paper from the Worldwatch Institute points out that buses and trains are fuel efficient *only* when the service is cheap, convenient, and comfortable enough to attract passengers at all times. A bus carrying nine passengers is much less energy efficient than a compact car carrying three people over the same distance.

Transportation patterns of the past 30 years seem to indicate that people prefer cars and planes over buses and trains. A car offers a person a freedom of mobility that can't be matched by any public transportation. In an automobile, a person is free from schedules and fixed routes. For long-distance travel, the car can't, of course, compete with a plane on speed. But neither can a bus or a train challenge air travel when time is important.

Over the past 30 years, the increases in the use of cars and planes in most developed countries have far outstripped increases in the use of buses and trains. This has been most noticeable in the U.S. Since World War II, as American car ownership rapidly increased, public transportation systems went through a remarkable decline.

A number of Americans have switched from cars and planes to buses and trains in recent years. But, in many cases the switch was made reluctantly. And, if given a choice, the people would switch back. Thousands of people commute to work by bus and train only because rush-hour traffic and city parking conditions make commuting by car costly and difficult.

On trips of a few hundred miles in length, the high cost of air travel and the delays caused by airport and airways have prompted people to switch to buses or trains for such travel. But again, in many cases, the switch was made reluctantly.

Many transportation planners insist that the appeal of mobility provided by the personal car and of high-speed long distance travel provided by the jet plane must be considered in the development of future systems.

Among predictions for the future are compact hybrid cars that can run on gasoline or electricity or a combination of both. Cal Tech's Jet Propulsion Lab is testing one now. Success of a hybrid car might lead to an efficient electric or solar-electric car. Several electric car types are being tested. But none seem ready for widespread use now.

Though a hybrid or an electric car may provide fuel economy and an easing of air pollution, neither development would do much to ease rush-hour congestion. Several suggestions have been put forward for mass transit systems in metropolitan areas. High on the list are high-speed trains similar to types in use in Japan and Europe. However, such systems are extremely expensive to build. And, many experts point out that if such systems are used primarily for rush-hour commuter traffic, they would never be energy-efficient or economical to operate. A mass-transit system must be appealing enough to attract passengers at all hours of service.

A number of U.S. cities are trying out compact buses on special lanes. And a number of people feel that various types of bus and trolley systems may be placed in use over the next ten years instead of large new subway systems.

Secretary of Transportation Lewis recently predicted, "I have a feeling that because of the cost of things, large, new subway systems will become a thing of the past in the next 20 years." And since the Department of Transportation controls federal aid for transportation, that could be considered more of a pronouncement than a prediction.

With fuel costs and automobile costs soaring, with highways crumbling, with mass-transit systems deteriorating, and with airways and airports becoming ever more congested, what's ahead for transportation in the U.S.? How will we get around ten years from now? Will cars and planes still dominate our system? If so, what types of cars will most people be driving? If not, what alternatives will we have?

BIBLIOGRAPHY

BOOKS, PAMPHLETS AND DOCUMENTS

Behrend, George. Luxury trains. Vendome. '81.

Bicycling Magazine Editors. Best bicycle tours. Rodale Press. '81.

Bowersox, Donald J. Introduction to transportation. Macmillan. '80.

Brown, Lester. Running on empty: the future of the automobile in an oil short world. Norton, '80.

Dunn, James A. Miles to go: European and American transportation policies. MIT Press. '81.

Fair, Marvin L. Transportation regulation. Dubuque: W. C. Brown. '79.

Fischler, Stanley I. Moving millions: an inside look at mass transit. Harper & Row. '79.

Friedlaender, Ann F. and Spady, Richard H. Freight transport regulation, equity, efficiency and competition in the rail and trucking industries. MIT Press. '81.

Hamilton, Neil and Hamilton, Peter. Governance of public enterprise: a case study of urban mass transit. Lexington Books. '81.

Harper, D. V. Transportation in America; users, carriers, government. Prentice-Hall, '78.

Hubbard, Freeman. Encyclopedia of North American railroading. McGraw-Hill. '81.

Moody's transportation manual, 1980.

Paaswell, Robert E. Problems of the carless. Praeger. '78.

Pederson, E. O. Transportation in cities. Pergamon. '80.

Roberts, Dick. Railroads: the case for nationalization. Pathfinder Press. '80.

Scheller, William G. Train trips: exploring America by rail. East Winds Press. '81.

Steiner, Henry M. Conflict in urban transportation. Lexington Books. '78.

U.S. Congress. House. Committee on the Budget. Task force on Transportation, Research and Development and Capital Resources. General views on transportation, R & D and capital improvements; hearings, March 16 and 19, 1981. 97th Congress. 1st Session. Supt. of Docs. Washington, D.C. 20515

U.S. Urban Mass Transportation Administration. Summary report of a survey of transportation handicapped users and non-users of special transportation systems in four cities. Washington, D.C. 20590. '80.

Vuchic, Vukan. Urban public transportation. Prentice-Hall. '81.

Wachs, Martin. Transportation for the elderly: changing lifestyles, changing needs. University of California Press, Berkeley. '79.

Wolfe, Fred. The bicycle: a commuting alternative. Signpost Book Pub. '79.

PERIODICALS

°AFL-CIO American Federationist. p 5–10. Je. '80. No-fare transit—a valuable experiment. Joe Brady.

Aging. 297:2–5. Jl. '79. Advocacy in this new age; public transportation issue and the aged. Maggie Kuhn.

American Planning Association Journal. 47:243–51. Jl. '81. Pricing urban transportation. Martin Wachs.

Annals of the American Academy of Political and Social Science. 453:70–95. Ja. '81. Transportation. Alan E. Pisarski.

Aviation Week & Space Technology. 110:27–8. My. 14, '79. Gasoline shortage could spur air traffic. J. M. Lenorovitz.

Aviation Week & Space Technology. 112:26–7. Ja. 21, '80. New U.S. policy may let wide-bodies in National.

Aviation Week & Space Technology. 116:26–7. Ja. 18, '82. Economic factors meld to cut aircraft buying. James Ott.

Aviation Week & Space Technology. 116:51+. Ja. 25, '82. Flat traffic, poor yields portend operating losses.

°Bicycling. p 55–62. Mr. '77. Bicycles for transportation. Dewey Chiesl.

Business Week. p 80+. N. 19, '79. Trailways; on its own in a drive to catch up with Greyhound.

Business Week. p 19. S. 1, '80. Commuter revolt that Conrail can't quell.

Business Week. p 106+. S. 15, '80. Flap over protectionism in mass transit.

Business Week. p 125+. S. 22, '80. Florida's test of truck deregulation.

Business Week. p 93–4. O. 27, '80. Are bicycle makers riding back to a boom?

Business Week. p 45–6. D. 29 '80/ Ja. 5, '81. Budget-cutting's first victim: mass transit (minifilibuster in Senate).

Business Week. p 58–9+. Jl. 20, '81. ICC nominations: a new deregulation test.

Business Week. p 64. Jl. 27, '81. Collision over subsidies.

*Changing Times. 35:60+. Ag. '81. Trollies, buses and ferries—great ways to see the sights.

Congressional Digest. 58:227+. O. '79. Evolution of motor carrier regulation.

Congressional Quarterly Weekly Report. 37:2289–91. O. 13, '79. Congress again faces rail money problems. Judy Sarasohn.

*Congressional Quarterly Weekly Report. 38:1505–9. My. 31, '80. Seven years later: equality for the handicapped. Harrison Donnelly.

Congressional Quarterly Weekly Report. 38:1804–5. Je. 28, '80. Senate votes to increase mass transit aid. Judy Sarasohn.

Current. p 30–8. N. '79. Future of the automobile.

*Dun's Review. 115:27–56. Ap. '80. Railroads: their impact on business in the coming decade. William H. Jones.

Economic Geography. 57:189–207. Jl. '81. Extended and internal commuting in the transformation of the intermetropolitan periphery. J. S. Fisher and R. L. Mitchelson.

Economist. 278:25. Ja. 10–16, '81. Cracks and chills.

Environment. 22:25–37. O. '80. Personal rapid transit. J. E. Anderson.

Environment and Behavior. 13:311–30. My. '81. Ridesharing programs: governmental response to urban transportation problems. D. D. Owens Jr.

Forbes. 123:41–2. Ap. 30, '79. Strange case of the kneeling bus; transbus. F. Schumer.

Forbes. 125:163–4+. Ja. 7, '80. Transportation.

Forbes. 125:108+. F. 18, '80. Mass transit—which is the right way to go? F. Schumer.

*Forbes. 127:122–3. Ap. 27, '81. "This place is a complete zoo." (I.C.C.) Barbara Rudolph.

Forbes. 128:83. Jl. 20, '81. They've been working on the railroad. Gerald Odening.

Forbes. 129:200–2. Ja. 4, '82. Railroads. A. D. Frank.

Forbes. 129:201. Ja. 4, '82. Connubial bliss, Southern style (Norfolk & Western-Southern Railway merger). A. D. Frank.

Fortune. 101:52–6+. Je. 2, '80. A comeback decade for the American car. Charles G. Burck.

Fortune. 103:58–60+. Mr. 9, '81. Bogged-down bus business. Lee Smith.

Futurist. p 171. Je. '78. Future of transit in the U.S.; some projections.

*Futurist. 15:59–63. D. '81. Railroads: out of the past and into the future. J. H. Foegen.

°Geographical Magazine. 53:511–16. My. '81. Long, long trail to work. J. O. Wheeler.

Geography. 53:245–9, Ja.; 318–33, F.; 374–80, Mr.; 450–4, Ap.; 511–16, My. '81. Transport in the USA.

Harpers. 262:14–15+. F. '81. Great transportation conspiracy. Jonathan Kwitny.

Intellect. p 442. Je. '77. Origins of the transportation cartel.

ITE Journal. 50:12–14. F. '80. Women in transportation. R. K. Pack.

ITE Journal. 51:51–5. Je. '81. Federal role in highway safety.

Journal of Economic History. 41:579–600. S. '81. Motorization and decline of urban public transit. D. J. St. Clair.

°Journal of the Institute of Socioeconomic Studies. VI, 2:34–37. Summer 1981. No free ride for U.S. mass transit manufacturers. William B. Ronan.

Journal of Social Issues. 37:31–50. Spring '81. Transportation energy conservation policy: implications for social science research. A. M. Zarega.

Monthly Labor Review. 102:58. Ap. '79. Has a labor protection law accelerated mass transit costs?

National Journal. 12:424–37. Mr. 15, '80. The auto: a prosperous past—a dubious future. Robert J. Samuelson.

National Journal. 12:1277–81. Ag. 2, '80. A new plan to target transit aid. R. L. Stanfield.

°Nation's Business. 67:34–6+. N. '79. Transportation 2000: how America will move its people and products; report of the National Transportation Policy Study Commission. J. H. Jennrich.

°Nation's Business. 67:36. N. '79. Ways of getting there.

New York Times. p B1. Ja. 5, '81. Rising crime in the subways.

New York Times. p A13. Ja. 6, '82. A safety improvement for the DC 10.

New York Times. p A3. Ja. 22, '82. Montreal transit strike ends after six days.

New York Times. p A1. Ja. 26, '82. A 25 percent fare increase for Connecticut commuters (Conrail).

New York Times. p B5. Ja. 26, '82. A Long Island Railroad mishap.

New York Times. p B3. F. 18, '82. Motorists protest proposed bridge and tunnel toll increases.

New York Times. p 26. F. 20, '82. A rise in the 30-cent PATH fare.

New York Times. p A1. F. 25, '82. A disputed tubing in subway stations.

New York Times. p B3. Mr. 5, '82. Transit labor talks opened.

New York Times. p B1. Mr. 9, '82. Foreign-made subway cars.

New York Times. p B1. Mr. 17, '82. Hundreds of commuters were trapped (PATH).

New York Times. p B1. Mr. 23, '82. The fare rate for medallion taxis barely covers expenses.

New York Times. p B1. Mr. 23, '82. The Japanese-made subway cars (Philadelphia).

New York Times. p 28. Mr. 28, '82. Dallas developers offer plan for financing transit system.

New York Times. p A18. Ap. 14, '82. A 25-state rail strike (Burlington-Northern System).

New Yorker. 55:23–4. S. 3, '79. Pumping pedals; rally for a car-free Central Park.

Newsweek. 95:63+. F. 25. '80. Green light on the rails.

Newsweek. 96:25. D. 22, '80. Mr. Fixit at transportation (A. L. Lewis to be Secretary).

Newsweek. 97:44–5. Je. 1, '81. Can't get there from here.

Public Policy. 12:341–67. Summer '81. Distribution of the tax burden of transit subsidies in the United States. John Pucher and Ira Hirschman.

Reader's Digest. 117:41–2+. S. '80. Where mass transit works. David Martindale.

*Saturday Review. 7:20–4. Ja. 5, '80. 80s traveler: his life and future times. Horace Sutton.

Science. 207:1337. Mr. 21, '80. Electrical science: the solution of municipal rapid transit (reprint from July 27, 1888 issue).

*Senior Scholastic. 114:8–11. O. 16, '81. How will you get around in 1991? S. F. O'Gorman.

*Sierra. 67:26+. Mr./Ap. '82. Transportation: The roads (and buses and trains) from here. Tom Downs and Neil Goldstein.

Smithsonian. 12:145–6+. My. '81. Confessions of a wayward bus connoisseur. Jim Lehrer.

Society. 10:39–42. Jl./Ag. '73. Public transportation and black unemployment. J. M. Goering and E. M. Kalachek.

Survey of Current Business. 61:29–34. My. '81. International travel and passenger fares. Joan E. Bolyard.

Technology Review. 82:54–9+. Ag/S. '80. Case for fuel-cell-powered vehicles. J. B. McCormick and J. R. Huff.

Technology Review. 83:80–81. Ja. '81. Urban transit: from one fad to the next.

Time. 114:52–4. Jl. 16, '79. Mess in mass transit.

*Time. 117:12–15. Mr. 30, '81. Rumbling toward ruin. Ellie McGrath.

Time. 117:14. Mr. 30, '81. Can anyone fx those Flxibles?

*Time. 118:25. Jl. 20, '81. Sick and inglorious transit.

Traffic Quarterly. 34:523–37. O. '80. Impact of transportation on the central business district. Kent A. Robertson.

Traffic Quarterly. 35:323–6. Jl. '81. Current issues facing transportation policymakers. Edward M. Whitlock.

°Transportation USA. 7:2–6. Fall '80. A transportation agenda for the 1980s.

U.S. News and World Report. 87:48–50. Jl. 2, '79. Changes in the way you will travel.

U.S. News and World Report. 87:50–2. Jl. 2, '79. City traffic: worse before it gets better.

°U.S. News and World Report. 87:38–40. D. 24, '79. How cities are coaxing people out of their cars.

U.S. News and World Report. 88:32–4. Je. 9, '80. Detroit fights back.

U.S. News and World Report. 89:78. O. 13, '80. A big step into the era of super-railroads.

U.S. News and World Report. 89:16. D. 22, '80. Transportation (new Secretary A. L. Lewis).

U.S. News and World Report. 90:11. Mr. 16, '81. Buses, subways face rough ride.

°U.S. News and World Report. 91:45. Jl. 20, '81. Equal access—it seemed like a good idea.

°U.S. News and World Report. 91:18–21. Ag. 31, '81. Great American transportation mess. Michael Doan.

U.S. News and World Report. 92:55–6. My. 3, '82. Conrail: one choo-choo that's making the grade. Fred W. Frailey.

USA Today. 107:48–50. Mr. '79. Deregulation or dewreckulation of interstate transportation? William Jacobs.

°USA Today. 110:54–6. N. '81. Public enterprise and public transportation. C. Kenneth Orski.

°Vital Speeches of the Day. 43:77–81. N. 15 '76. Autos and mass transit. Daphne Christensen.

Vital Speeches of the Day. 46:315–18. Mr. 1, '80. Role of regulatory agencies in the eighties. Leslie Kanuk.

Vital Speeches of the Day. 46:367–71. Ap. 1, '80. Transportation policy. W. T. Coleman.

Wall Street Journal. 197:56. Ap. 2, '81. End of line? Mass transit is facing a financial crisis.

°Washington Monthly. 12:51–8. Ap. '80. Where are you, Benito, now that we need you? Graham Beene.